Risk, Challenge and Adventu

What is the difference between 'risk' and 'danger'? What can children learn from taking risks? How can you provide key experiences for children and ensure their safety outdoors?

Young children will naturally seek out challenges and take risks and this is crucial to their overall development. This book clearly explains why children should be given the freedom to take risks and provides practical guidance on how to offer stimulating and challenging outdoor experiences that will extend all areas of children's learning.

Including examples of activities for all weather conditions across all areas of learning, the book covers:

- the pedagogical history of adventure, risk and challenge;
- health, wellbeing and keeping safe;
- the adult role;
- risk assessment;
- supporting individual children with different needs;
- environments that enable challenging and adventurous play;
- working with parents and addressing concerns;
- observation, planning and assessment.

This book is essential reading for practitioners and students who wish to provide rich experiences for children that will enable them to become confident and adventurous learners.

Kathryn Solly is the retired Headteacher of Chelsea Open Air Nursery School and Children's Centre. She is now a specialist Early Years consultant, trainer and author.

Risk, Challenge and Adventure in the Early Years

A practical guide to exploring and extending learning outdoors

Kathryn Solly

Routledge
Taylor & Francis Group

LONDON AND NEW YORK

First published 2015
by Routledge
2 Park Square, Milton Park, Abingdon, Oxon OX14 4RN

Simultaneously published in the USA and Canada
by Routledge
711 Third Avenue, New

Routledge is an impri

© 2015 Kathryn Solly

British Library Cata
A catalogue record f

Library of Congress
Solly, Kathryn.
Risk, challenge and adventure in the early years / Kathryn Solly.
pages cm
Includes bibliographical references and index.
1. Education, Preschool. I. Title.
LB1140.2.S673 2015
372.21--dc23
2014028366

ISBN: 978-0-415-66739-5 (hbk)
ISBN: 978-0-415-66740-1 (pbk)
ISBN: 978-0-203-81707-0 (ebk)

Typeset in Celeste
by Saxon Graphics Ltd, Derby

Printed and bound in the United States of America by Publishers Graphics,
LLC on sustainably sourced paper.

Contents

Preface

Throughout my unorthodox career in teaching I have had many opportunities cross-phase to witness how crucial the environment within which children and young people learn is to the quality of their education. I have taught in the secondary, primary and nursery phases, and have experience with young people in a Pupil Referral Unit, a special school and several mainstream environments too. My personal interest in playing and learning outdoors as a child was enhanced when I started my teaching career in secondary education on Voluntary Service Overseas in Papua New Guinea leading eventually to headship today where my team and I provide high quality learning challenges for young children under the age of 5, both indoors and out, every day at Chelsea Open Air. I believe that my own ability nurtured in childhood gave me the ability to wisely risk take, be resourceful and be creative out-of-doors and this has gone on to influence how I teach as well as my leadership style and passion for high quality early years education and care.

Growing up in the late 1950s and 60s, I thought nothing of going across the fields with my sister and friends, often with a dog or two for company. As I grew up I had opportunities to create a rope swing over a stream, cook (badly) on a small bonfire and build dens for all sorts of imaginative play. My parents were not neglectful and knew roughly where we would be, but trusted us, our community and our environment to give us a natural childhood as they knew we would be home hungry for our next meal. We did not have mobile phones to keep in touch and got little sympathy if we got nettle rash, scratched by brambles or told off by a neighbour from whose garden we may have 'borrowed' flowers to bring home. In many ways learning out-of-doors was the norm when I was a child and still is in many cultures and countries around the world. Many people have recognised that playing outdoors is often more enjoyable for children than playing indoors, because they have more freedom from adult intervention and because it is about real life experience.

Over my adult lifetime the perspective in England has become increasingly driven by concerns over safety and fear of hazards both seen and unseen. This 'cotton wool' risk-averse culture has expanded over the last 16 years, leading to the removal of many of the normal, hands-on outdoor play opportunities for children that I grew up with. However, gradually over the last few years there has been a slow change and retaliation against the media maelstrom of health and safety paranoia. Thankfully this has provided a huge

Preface

resurgence of interest in providing real opportunities for adventure, risk and challenge for children. There have also been indications that if children are denied the opportunity to develop these skills and use them in the environment, they will not develop the resilience, independence and creativity they need for adulthood, therefore having long-term implications for their future development, health and wellbeing as well as on society.

Through my own learning and teaching experience with people from birth to 75, I have widened my perspectives of what is learning and what is teaching and how outdoor education in its many forms can be useful. I have come to wonder whether outdoor education is the equivalent of teaching outdoors and/or learning outdoors. In many ways I know my perspective has moved from the former to the latter as I (and many others) am happier learning (and teaching) outdoors. Thank you to the numerous young children, colleagues and families who have helped grow my adventure in learning about risk and challenge. Our daughter chose to spend her tenth birthday in a bivouac at Childe Beale Trust with about ten friends. They collected and chopped the wood for their fire and cooked a fry-up very ably as if this was everyday practice, before snuggling up together on a very frosty March night not far from the Thames. Children are growing up in a world which places greater demands on them in terms of self-control, restricted freedom, variable values and less real fun as their lives are programmed by routines and adult agendas. The creative and intelligent individuals we are going to need to solve the world's problems in the future will only be able to rise to such challenges if the liberal attitudes they learn as young children are both creative and imaginative so that each child's physical prowess expands alongside their independence and self-belief.

So this is my starting point: young children are unique, active and creative learners who need the very best positive learning environments and opportunities with and without adults. This book tells much of my learning journey and passionate belief that everyday opportunities to learn outside are essential for a wide range of life skills to emerge and develop such as leadership, resourcefulness, environmental respect and understanding, collaboration and creativity. These I believe can only occur through real opportunities for adventure, risk and challenge in the early years.

Dedication and acknowledgement

For my initial interest in outdoors I have to thank my country childhood and my parents Irene and Roy for giving me the opportunities to experience adventure, risk and challenge naturally. They taught me a knowledge and love of plants, gardening and wildlife as well as to value and respect my fellow human companions. This eventually translated into a degree in Environmental Science and a successful teaching career in sharing this same love with children and young people. They also supported my adventures to Papua New Guinea and later, now a wife and mother, to Albania.

Thank you also to my husband George, and children Huw, Ralph and Imogen who also help to inspire and extend my learning about outdoors through their own lives. Another thank you must go to all the children whom I have had the privilege of teaching, their families, my colleagues from whom I have learnt so much, and professional friends, especially Barbara Isaacs, Anne Nelson, Professor Tina Bruce, Chris Whelan, Sue Allingham, Patsy Wagner and Chris Watkins who have inspired, challenged and encouraged me.

I would also like to acknowledge the help and guidance of Annamarie Kino who has shared my journey.

Publisher's acknowledgement

All images courtesy of Siren Films ©

Introduction

Susan Isaacs was one of the two founders of Chelsea Open Air Nursery in the 1920s. She believed in the crucial importance of play and was especially interested in children's emotional lives. Her observation-based practice was central to her work and she saw it as a means of affording attention, respect and systematic study of all that children do. Isaacs researched how, with gentle guidance and detailed observation and reflection, adults could best support children's learning without the need for harsh words or punishments. Isaacs was very influential on education during the early twentieth century and was the first to provide a climbing frame for young children. The Maltings School in Cambridge and Chelsea Open Air had school rooms opening out onto the garden with a sandpit, see-saw, climbing frame and plots for each child to grow vegetables. Children were allowed to use adult tools such as doubled-handed tree saws to encourage co-operation, a real typewriter, Bunsen burners and a microscope. Susan Isaacs (1932: 170) advocated the development of children's problem solving skills by extending their 'native interest in things and people around them – the street, the market, the garden, the railway, the world of plants and animals'. She was also aware of the risks involved in her comments (120) by emphasising 'some degree of understanding the world around him since he has to live in it, and to live safely.' She was however, not foolhardy and created simple practical rules with the children for their safety such as only one child on the shed roof at any time! She continued to stress the practical need for environmental exploration:

> The thirst for understanding goes beyond the mere practical safeguarding of bodily survival. It springs from the child's deepest emotional needs and with the intelligent child a veritable passion. He must know and master the world to make it feel safe.
>
> (113)

The opportunity to be outdoors was essential for children then and Isaacs gave the children aged between 2 and 10 years of age an unusual degree of freedom to explore outside and indoors too. In her garden there was a range of pets including snakes, silkworms and salamanders. She gave the children rich opportunities to investigate in depth and think carefully about biological and spiritual concepts including death. She recorded the children requesting to dig up the pet rabbit several weeks after its demise which she proceeded to do. When reading her books it is fascinating how many such

Introduction

events have occurred in my own experience with young children at Chelsea Open Air to this day. We promise parents during the induction meeting that we will answer children's questions about birth, death, sex and excretion in an open, honest and developmentally appropriate way.

Leading a nursery school where Isaacs was the pioneering force is a real privilege and it comes with an enormous responsibility to stay true to the important ethos she created. Today our children still choose for themselves to learn inside or out for 48 weeks of the year. They enjoy role-play with real china and cutlery, woodwork, sewing, cooking and gardening with real tools as well as expeditions into the community to extend their interests and satisfy their needs in small groups just like Isaacs' (1930: 288–89) 'excursions' which were 'taken at all seasons of the year.'

Today we regularly have visitors at Chelsea Open Air who often ask us questions such as these:

- 'Have you heard about the school that stopped doing the egg and spoon race in case someone dropped an egg and someone was allergic to it?'
- 'What about conkers? Do your children wear protective eye goggles?'
- 'Do you allow pets, woodwork, hoses and bonfires?'
- 'How can your children be left to play with those ladders?'
- 'Do you go outside to play when it rains, snows or is frosty?'
- 'How do you sleep at night?'

This book aims to inspire practitioners to reflect upon their pedagogy and practice outside and improve it still further alongside the provision of some tried and tested means to get outside with young children and do something different. It is based upon experience, recognised good practice and educational research. It also includes important pedagogical background to build both practitioners understanding and confidence of risk, challenge and adventure in different contexts and support them in involving colleagues and parents in this exciting learning journey.

The book starts by looking at the pioneers of education and their influence on risk, challenge and adventure in the early years. It then goes on to explore the concepts of risk, challenge and adventure in the early years and consider how these relate to early years education today and the benefits of outdoor play. This is followed by the different attitudes to risk, challenge and adventure in the early years. Later chapters offer practical guidance and background on the role of the adult and the environment and the resources used outside. The book moves on to discuss the benefits and practicalities of expeditions outside the setting. Finally there is practical guidance on how to plan adventurous activities throughout the year. By the end of the book it is hoped that you will feel inspired to go outdoors with young children and do something different, confident that your practice is firmly underpinned by pedagogical understanding of risk, challenge and adventure.

CHAPTER 1

The historical background

This chapter tells a brief history of the pioneers of education from Comenius to Margaret McMillan and how they have given us clear foundations as to the importance and value of adventure, risk and challenge in the early years. It pays particular attention to the work and influence of Dr Susan Isaacs and the 'open air' movement. Finally, it finishes by considering more recent influences on risk and challenge and the lasting impact of the pioneers on quality early years provision.

The early pioneers

John Comenius

Educational experiences involving risk, challenge and adventure began with John Comenius (1592–1670) who was the originator of the concept of natural education and what could be achieved by learning holistically through all the senses. This remains a cornerstone in education today in many countries. Comenius was also the first to suggest education for girls.

Jean-Jacques Rousseau

It is perhaps Rousseau (1712–78) whom many would claim first created the image of the free child in terms of nurturing children's growth. This is evident in the child's ability to make informed decisions about choices in their free play and in particular their natural play. This enhances healthy living through genuine activity and supports every area of a child's development.

Johann Pestalozzi and Robert Owen

Like Rousseau, Swiss pioneer Pestalozzi (1746–1827) believed that education 'must be according to nature.' Their influence led to the likes of Robert Owen (1771–1858) establishing his nursery school in Scotland within the workplace at New Lanark in 1816. Whilst being an engineer of social change, Owen influenced opinions to oppose child labour and to ensure that children were happier and well treated. His workers' children were encouraged to spend hours playing outside and there was a strong emphasis on physical activity.

Friedrich Froebel

Friedrich Froebel (1782–1852) grew up in Germany with a strong interest in nature and was an apprentice forester as a young man. He was influenced by the writings of Rousseau and Pestalozzi and also worked in a Swiss orphanage. It was this post that sparked his interest in play, child development and child-centred education in the early years. He created his first kindergarten (children's paradise garden) to reflect his philosophy about young children, stressing that children should primarily be allowed to be children. Froebel was also passionate about the inter-connectedness of life and its transformational qualities. The garden (both communal and individual) was at the centre of his work with young children. He emphasised first-hand experience with nature, music, spirituality, the arts and mathematics. His children were encouraged, rather than made, to garden and go on nature walks as these gave them more freedom to learn. This led to a progressive movement throughout the twentieth century for education to involve aspects of spirituality, respect, care, physicality and natural independence as well as the emergence of the value of the imagination, music and dance in learning.

Rudolf Steiner

One of the famous influencers to this day on nursery education was Rudolf Steiner (1861–1925). He wanted to create an education to give children the ability to think clearly and with a sensitivity of feeling, willingness and imagination, by fostering personal and social development through the rhythm of the day and the seasons. In Wilkinson's book about Steiner (1980: 6) the child is described as accepting the environment and drinking it in, which demonstrates the value placed upon real life experience. He was strongly against forcing learning and seeing it in subject areas but valued the spoken word, stories and creativity. He also valued play and the imagination as being highly supportive of child development at the child's natural pace and hence the printed word was not introduced until the age of 7. His schools provided, and still provide a strong emphasis on gardening, cooking, cleaning and learning from adult role models with such skills as baking bread, carving wood and carrying out daily tasks. He felt that young children do not experience the same distance and separation from the world that adults do because they are constantly observing. Hence they use this same intensity of observation to feed their play with ideas and use objects symbolically and are much more aware of what we would describe today as mood. This means the children often act out scenes from their daily lives, say, by getting the dolls up and dressed when they first come into the kindergarten to making the bread dough on baking day. Clouder and Rawson (1998: 36) describe this in their book about Waldorf Education as 'Play is the serious work of childhood.'

Maria Montessori

Pioneer Maria Montessori (1870–1952), having read a great deal about education across the world, wanted to make a difference for vulnerable children with special and individual needs. She established the Casa dei Bambini in the slums of Rome as part of what now would be described as urban regeneration. She based her work on scientific observation and focused on children learning through their senses and through movement in an environment designed to meet their needs. She referred to the child as 'a little explorer'. Gardening, gymnastics, caring for pets and freedom of choice to follow their interests within fairly long periods of uninterrupted time with only a few adult boundaries were the norm in her nurseries. She also introduced child-sized furniture.

The later pioneers

Margaret and Rachel McMillan

Friedrich Froebel, and later John Dewey (1859–1952) with his central vision, 'I believe that education therefore is a process of living and not preparation for future living' (1897), certainly influenced Margaret McMillan (1860–1931) who is credited with inventing the nursery school and placing great emphasis upon the importance of the garden, wholesome food, baths, fresh air, light and regular sleep/exercise periods to improve children's health and wellbeing in the slums of Deptford. She shocked the middle classes at the time as to the ill health of poor children and set up nurseries and camps to improve their health and nurture them. In 1914 McMillan wrote:

> Children want space at all ages, but from the ages of one to seven, space, that is ample space, is almost as much wanted as food and air. To move, to run, to find things out by new movement, to feel one's life in every limb, that is the life of early childhood.

Margaret went on to create an extensive and beautiful garden with shelter provided by a variety of trees and bushes, terraced rock gardens, a sensory herb garden, a vegetable garden for the children's meals, as well as cultivating wild flowers. It also had climbing equipment, sandpits and 'the heap', where children could explore natural and manufactured objects. She was very aware of the adult's moral responsibility to provide the best outdoor experience, as is seen in her comment: 'How often in later life, will their thoughts go back to the first garden, which surely must be as rich as we can make it.' (McMillan, in Bradford Education, 1995: 8).

Grace Owen

In 1923 Grace Owen was also to recognise the importance of natural things and real life experience: 'There will be no set lessons, but the children will live as far as possible with nature. School pets, as is well recognised, either as residents or visitors, give children much valuable experience.'

The historical background

Susan Isaacs

Dr Isaacs (1885–1948) was a Froebelian (an advocate of social and political change) who became interested in the work of Montessori, Dewey, Piaget and Melanie Klein. She was a fascinating woman and was in many ways ahead of her time. She had an enquiring mind and used many of their ideas to create her particular philosophy which celebrated:

- the natural curiosity of children;
- the importance of the underlying unity of nature and its relationships with children, families and staff; and
- the law of opposites and that theory must always have practice and vice versa.

Isaacs understood that if professionals understand children, then this could help advance their learning. As she sought to understand children, she became a great narrative recorder by meticulously observing children's play, or as she termed it watching 'children in the real.'

She found out that children were:

- Discoverers
- Reasoners
- Thinkers

and so children were encouraged to express themselves by asking questions and stating their opinions, showing their feelings and following their individual interests in a rich learning environment indoors and out. She was systematic in her observations and always involved children's families. By today's standards the education provided by Isaacs was as she said 'relatively free' and took the form of an 'all round lessening of the degree of inhibition of children's impulses' compared to other schools of the period (Isaacs 1930: 12).

The other aspect of these 'relatively free' conditions was the physical environment – the children were led to be more active, more curious, more creative, more exploratory and more inventive. They were allowed to move freely indoors and out and had access to the outdoors to pet animals, harvest fruit trees, use scientific equipment such as Bunsen burners, microscopes and dissecting tools, real bricks for building, a space for bonfires, and a see-saw with hooks underneath so weights could be fitted for weighing activities on a larger scale. She also used small child-sized furniture, real china and dressing-up clothes as advocated by Montessori. There was also a lathe and woodworking equipment, and cupboards full of Montessori's equipment.

The 'Open Air' movement

The development of the open air schools dates back to the ancient Greeks as well as the more familiar pioneers Rousseau and Froebel. Margaret McMillan was the English educational pioneer who, with her sister Rachel, played a leading role in establishing the Nursery School movement in Britain as well as improving the health and care of young children. Much of their vision has been carried out by today's children's centres. Through their lengthy campaigning they established the first Open Air Nursery School in Deptford in 1911. The benefits of such schools were to:

- nip disease in the bud;
- prevent sequential disease;
- provide opportunities for the body to mend and repair following illness or accident;
- nurture debilitated children; and
- promote modern methods of education, i.e. learning by doing.

Thus they had several fundamental principles:

- fresh air and sunlight
- proper diet
- rest or quiet play
- hygienic ways of living
- individual attention
- medical treatment
- special educational methods.

From 1912 the Board of Education showed its approval of these schools by paying a special grant of £3 per head under part 11 of the Medical Treatment Grant Regulations. This meant that when Chelsea Open Air opened in 1928 to 13 children they had regular access to a doctor who examined them and gave advice on diet and hygiene. It was founded with the intention to provide for all children regardless of income and gradually a wide cross-section of society began to attend. Frequent concerns for parents were of a practical nature such as table manners, swearing and other children's germs! A strict regime of sunlight, fresh air and medication led to a drop in illnesses and an increase in attendance from 71% in 1935 to 89% in 1937.

Susan Isaacs realised how crucial access to outdoor space was in learning as she comments:

> Little children need space, both for their physical efforts and so that they shall not be much in each other's way and annoy each other by contact or noise. To be boxed up in a small nursery is a very trying experience for vigorous, healthy children of three to five years of age and a great source of irritation and nervous strain. Space in itself has a calming and beneficial effect.'
>
> (1954: 29)

This latter factor is even more critical today.

Isaacs (1932) also stressed the value of spontaneous play in developing:

- the joy of movement whilst perfecting bodily skills;
- genuine interest in real things and events in the world around them; and
- real love of make-believe and acting out the world that children see.

Chelsea Open Air

Chelsea Open Air Nursery School was founded by Dr Susan Isaacs in 1928 with funding from American benefactress Natalie Davies so her two children could attend and benefit.

The historical background

In a building dating from 1587, the open air ethos was part of a countrywide movement in the 1920s which recognised the importance of engaging children's learning in the fresh air. It was also linked to the awareness of creativity and imagination ushered forth by the Arts and Crafts movement. It was realised then that many children did not have enough access to fresh air, sunlight and exercise for their healthy development – a problem still prevalent today. More recently we built upon this ethos further when the children's centre was added in 2006. To this day, indoors and out, we still try to build upon the pedagogical strengths and practices of Susan Isaacs in recording children's learning journeys which Isaacs established in her observational writing and clear fascination with real children and their social relationships when she wrote about being interested in 'everything that little children do and feel.'

Recent influences on adventure, risk and challenge

The Haddow and Plowden Reports

There is a clear link to these pioneers in the creation of the Haddow Report published in 1933 on Nursery and Infant Schools, and later in the Plowden Report in 1967 as to how children should learn and be taught with a strong emphasis in following their interests indoors and out so that education was not 'disembodied'.

Lady Allen of Hurtwood

In a book entitled *Planning for Play*, Lady Allen of Hurtwood (1968: 43–44) described nursery schools as the ideal solution in the provision of play for children aged between 2 to 5 years. She commented, however, that there are 'still too few of them' but goes on to give examples such as Kingswood Nursery School in Dulwich:

> Outside, there is a covered play-space, store room for equipment, and a large sandpit. The layout of the gardens forms an integral design; there is a grass mound for the children to run up and down, which was made out of the surplus soil from the building operations. Rough ground among the trees has been left as an adventure area.

Later (1968: 64–77) she describes the adventure playground at Notting Hill, an area which 'is densely populated and under privileged on a site of just over an acre given and fenced by the borough' with its separate area for under-fives. This was focused on the playhouse as a favourite 'roaming space' for the group. It was recognised that they needed 'their own very small-scale environment' linked to imaginative play.

> A group of five-year-olds (girls and boys) spent a good hour making "mud pies" in the playhouse, but the sand to make them was brought in a paper bag from the sandpit, the water from the fountain, the "fruit" (sawdust) from the "arena" where sawing had been done, the "frosting" was shaken from an old can of cleaning powder.

Lady Hurtwood (1968: 18–21) also describes using powerful photographs of the slow progression of playgrounds from what she terms the 'prison period', i.e. iron structures such as slides, swings etc., to the 'concrete period', to the 'novelty period', citing a defunct steam traction engine as a piece of play equipment. She continues onwards to the 'maze period' and finally the 'do-it-yourself period', showing how children, if left alone, can do it for themselves. She cites some clear but simple design advice which could be well employed today.

Very recent developments

The recent advent of books such as *The Dangerous Book for Boys* (Iggulden and Iggulden 2006) and *An Outdoor Book for Girls* (Beard 2007; first published in 1915) are proving very popular with many families alongside activity centres providing holidays and school journeys where children can build rafts, ride ponies, learn to kayak or try archery often for the first time. The television series led by celebrity choir master Gareth Malone in his *Extraordinary School for Boys* even found agreement with many teachers that certain groups of children need different experiences to excite their interest and 'turn them onto learning.' This programme sought over eight weeks to demonstrate how 'risk, challenge, physical activity and immediacy' (Millard 2010) when provided at Pear Tree Mead Primary School in Harlow, Essex would start to change the perspectives of the boys so they would be readier to learn and, in particular, improve their literacy levels by 6 months. Malone provided many creative outdoor options including den making, camp fires and camping overnight in the school grounds with dads.

Conclusion

The pioneers have had a great impact upon establishing the quality foundations of young children's play and learning both indoors and outdoors. We have a great deal to learn and reflect upon in how their practice can influence us today. It is our task as practitioners to understand their messages and to ensure that they are adapted and taken forward wisely and established daily in our provision and practice so they benefit young children now and in years to come.

CHAPTER 2

Defining adventure, risk and challenge

Introduction

Adventure, risk and challenge in the early years are not new concepts as illustrated by Margaret McMillan (1930) who described her ideal outside play area:

> A little children's garden must offer every kind of inducement to muscular play and action. It must be planned with an eye to real safety whilst encouraging children to play bravely and adventurously. Rough stones, narrow curved paths, jumping-off places and a grassy stretch to lie on.

This chapter looks at the conceptual ideas behind adventure, challenge and risk taking in the early years. It examines what we mean by these terms in the context of early years education. There is also an in-depth look at 'flow' and how important it is in terms of risk, challenge and adventure for children's life experience.

Explaining the concepts

The *Oxford University Press Compact Dictionary Online* (2011) defines adventure as 'an exciting or very unusual experience' or 'an unusual and exciting or daring experience'. This seems balanced and in line with my view. Whereas the definition of risk, on the other hand, is negative and is very closely associated with hazard: 'A situation involving exposure to danger'. Hazard, meanwhile, is defined as 'a danger or risk' or 'a potential source of danger.' The definition of challenge is more balanced: 'A task or situation that tests someone's abilities.'

What do we mean by challenging play?

Challenging play is something which young children thirst for and create by themselves if given the chance. It is very personal, individual and unique to each child but also may involve small groups of children who share common interests playing alongside each other or starting to collaborate in creating their own particular challenge. Challenges can also be created by observant practitioners who know just what equipment or resource to provide so that individuals or small groups can take their next steps with little direct adult involvement – just an observant eye. For example, many children will try to jump or climb further or higher without any adult intervention. Others may, due to their individual abilities, needs, interests and passions, need more individual support or guidance in their search to find more mini-beasts or perhaps create a kite or streamer to chase around the garden with. Children need challenging play whether indoors or outside.

All children at one time or another need to have the experience of challenge within their play and learning in order to move forward. For many this will be self-initiated. At other times the same child may need a practitioner to provide a nudge, a word of encouragement or a different piece of equipment at that crucial point in time in order that they are challenged.

Sound planning combined with child-initiated learning and well-thought through and cleverly designed activities can advance children's individual holistic growth physically, intellectually, socially and emotionally. This can be as varied as learning to put your coat and boots on for yourself, to tree climbing, hiding in bushes, standing on top of a hill and rolling down it or racing through a tunnel shouting at the top of your voice. However, as each child is unique, real challenge can only be individually described as moving into the 'stretch zone'. This is the area which, if you are pushing your own boundaries, lays between your 'comfort zone' and at the opposing end your 'panic zone'. Thus going out on an expedition may make one child feel excited, another slightly anxious and a third will be pressing the alarm button loud and hard! It can have a similar effect on their parents, staff and carers too. Going out into the world to somewhere new, mastering a new skill, learning how to use a new piece of equipment or coping with a new routine when a special visitor comes, all allow children to make discoveries about themselves, enhance their wellbeing and build knowledge, skills and understanding. Much comes down to the intuition and instinct of well-trained practitioners intervening or holding back at those critical points in each child's development.

Figure 2.1 Climbing higher!
Image taken from *The Power of Physical Play* © Siren Films Ltd (2014).

What is adventurous play?

Adventurous play is about the richness of young children's imaginations and interests and how we nurture these so they have the time, spaces, resources and environments to creatively take their learning forward themselves. In the early years, adventure at the adult-led level is not about inappropriate or hazardous activities such as map reading, bivouacking, abseiling etc., but more about the smaller-scale experiences often outside in the fresh air like cooking in a fire bowl, grooming a pony in the garden or going on an expedition to Forest School.

Adventure at the child-led level can mean, for example, creating a den, a rocket or a castle with a variety of pieces of fabric and a few crates, A-frames or similar equipment. This could be alongside the adult-led experience of carving pumpkins to make Jack-o-Lanterns in the autumn harvest.

What is crucial is doing something different in one way or another and providing an opportunity for extended experience as children develop in the areas of collaboration with others, problem solving, in-depth thought and reflection. There are real educational opportunities to be gained if young children have the freedom to initiate adventures themselves, appropriately supported by staff within an enabling environment.

What is risk-taking?

The term 'risk-taking' is used and often misused generally to support negativity or used loosely lacking real definition and purpose. Some documents such as the *Statutory Framework for the Early Years Foundation Stage* (DfES 2007) refer to 'reasonable risk-taking', meaning that the adult knows and understands the risks but assesses the likelihood of harm being low, taking into consideration the age and stage of development of the children. On the website Learning Outside the Classroom (www.lotc.org.uk) it states 'a small risk of minor injury is not considered significant' as one factor in a risk assessment but more than one would require an assessment strategy to be in place.

Risk-taking in the context of this book is grounded in the things which young children and adults often choose to do daily. It is about doing that little bit more, doing something differently, or exploring somewhere you haven't been before. Examples might include pushing yourself to take one more step up the ladder on the climbing frame when you first come to nursery, balancing without holding an adult's hand across a self-made bridge of planks and crates or managing to silently maintain your involvement in observing a butterfly feeding from a flower even though you are desperate to ask a question. It is something that is individual but could involve potential hazard or loss if not established within a context of appropriate risk-taking in a relatively 'safe' environment.

The importance of flow

The author who really discovered the inherent value in the importance of adventure, risk and challenge is the Czech psychologist Csikszentmihalyi in his concept of 'flow'. He has reasoned that as personalities we are rewarded when we are challenged and deeply engaged in an experience or activity and opposingly we are de-motivated in life experiences when they are boring, run of the mill and not the things we enjoy in work, play or relationships. Flow usually happens when someone's skills are concentrated in overcoming a challenge which is just about feasible for them. If the challenge is too great, they become frustrated and even stressed. If the challenge is seen as low, the effort involved depreciates and apathy is likely to follow and the task often not completed. Flow is very evident in sports and adventure activities when, for example, climbers or swimmers are challenged to provide just that bit more in terms of height or speed. A singer might find flow when using a fuller range of their voice, as might the surgeon who has to perform an operation involving different procedures. Csikszentmihalyi described flow as 'flashes of intense living against the dull background of life' (1997: 31).

Flow demands a person's complete attention and focus – there is no space for distracting thoughts or feelings and time passes without the person noticing as everything in their mind and body is stretched to capacity. Therefore work and play for adults (as hobbies), and young people and children is far more satisfying when flow is achieved. The joy of outdoor activities is that flow is clearly more evident. Adults tend to impose fewer curriculum restrictions, and as a result the children benefit. Flow tends to 'act as a magnet for learning – that is, developing new levels of challenges and skills' (1997: 33). Flow nurtures real learning experiences and enhances dispositions which are essential for young children in their whole lives. Too much provision of low grade maintenance activities within the early years leads to boredom and apathy and too much stimulation can lead to anxiety, stress and worry.

So how do we ensure each child achieves the right level of flow? This can be done by observing carefully to see when children are happiest and most motivated. What do they talk about? Who do they engage with? How long do they focus? Armed with this evidence, we as adults can engineer a creative tapestry from which children can select, and thus have some ownership of, in order to achieve an appropriate experience of flow. We start with their interests and strengths and cannily extend their learning into wider spheres as they thirst for new adventures and challenges. If we provide learning experiences where children have to interact with one another, this will lead to further encounters of flow, as being friends provides more positive experiences.

The importance of play

Teenagers are often happiest when they are away from adults and engaged in what motivates them, often finding flow in situations of self-challenge. Young children, because of their age and vulnerability, need to be far more closely engaged with adults, but they still need adventures, challenges and the real opportunity to learn about risk-taking. Through such experiences they come to understand their own capabilities and how they can make judgements as to what they can or cannot do in controlled circumstances, as Cook and Heseltine (1998: 4) discuss in their research. It is therefore critical that we allow young children to play as it is the 'perfect vehicle', as Lally (1991: 72–74) points out, for them to 'explore, discover, construct, repeat and consolidate, represent, create, imagine, socialise.'

In schools, play-based learning is enhanced by knowledgeable adults. Children need quality time to learn to play initially, then through close observation and interaction with them, adults can fine-tune children's experiences by feeding in ideas and pointing out resources which they might wish to use. Finally, adults can act as catalysts to play by giving children appropriate challenges to ensure play flows effectively with no one agenda dominating so all the children, whatever their stage of development, can extend and grow through the experience. This gives the children time to think, and to become confident in their play as a means to share, solve problems, and collaborate via sustained shared thinking with sensitive adults.

Bringing adventure, risk and challenge together

We are trying to create what Abbott and Nutbrown (2001: 112) describe as a 'palette of opportunities' by using experiences outside of the indoor classroom for a wide range of young children.

Learning through adventure, risk and challenge helps children develop a rich array of abilities, skills and understanding to cope, problem solve and make informed choices. It also helps children take responsibility for the consequences of their decision-making from activities in the classroom, when meeting visitors, out in the school grounds and out and about on expeditions into the local community. Learning to plan for factors such as weather, transport, meals, time of day, and other people helps them to understand the management of risk and hazard. 'Exposure to well managed risks helps children learn important life skills, including how to manage risks for themselves ... children, in particular need to learn to manage risks, and adventure activities ... are an ideal way of doing this' (HSE 2007).

Unless we give our children genuine experience of adventure, risk and real challenge our society will suffer. This exploratory view is supported by Guy Claxton (1990) who argues that to be creative you have 'to dare to be different', 'to live on the edge' rather than accepting what is given.

CHAPTER 3

Attitudes towards risk, challenge and adventure

Introduction

This chapter looks at attitudes to risk, challenge and adventure and how things have changed for better or worse. It will discuss the current risk-averse culture and the fact that children appear to be playing outside less. It explores the move to more formal learning at an earlier age alongside the loss of play outdoors. Moving on, this chapter focuses on the factors which lessen play outdoors such as our risk-averse culture, increasing urbanisation and the marketisation of childhood. Finally, it moves on to the positive attitudes that are becoming apparent through Forest Schools and the involvement of bodies such as the National Trust as well as the influence of other countries

Changing perceptions

When I have asked adults about their memories of their own childhood play, whether recalling a childhood in the countryside or an urban one, they mention a range of experiences which they remember clearly:

- mixed age groups;
- gardening;
- freedom to roam only returning to eat or sleep;
- imaginative play in dens, trees and using props;
- messy play such as mud pies, petal 'perfume' and damming streams;
- construction with locally found materials;
- games with rules like hop scotch, hide and seek, jacks;
- physical play including rough and tumble.

It seems that adults remember and genuinely treasure these experiences from their own childhood. So why does it now seem that many feel prevented from providing similar opportunities for young children – and if this is the case, why is it occurring? Is it a result of misconceptions from the media? Or is it that society now expects children to spend less time playing outside because there are other more easily managed options indoors?

After the 1950s and 60s the value placed on natural play outdoors began to change and there was shorter time devoted to it for nursery and reception children. This was possibly a result of improving living circumstances after the war. It may also have resulted from changing attitudes towards the value of formal schooling at an earlier age alongside major changes in the working patterns of mothers and fathers which required more child care. There has certainly been far greater influence of the media on child rearing and the rapid pace of technological change has resulted in the media being more present in our everyday lives than ever before. We appear as a result to have a paradox between trust and control in child rearing. Social media in particular means we are so well informed and connected that a kind of false intimacy has developed around child rearing, rather than the more disparate relationships and slower communication methods of previous generations. Then, families really knew their communities and more people were involved in teaching children how to behave within them. Now, families are further removed and, due to an overload of up-to-the-minute information via the media, often disengage with family/community involvement and their associated responsibilities.

The move to more formal learning

Within formal schooling for children aged 5 years and older, playtime and similar activity periods was supervised by a minimum of staff so the remaining staff could enjoy a break. It had little relationship to the real needs of children. Playtime was regarded as a social and physical time for children to let off steam before returning to concentrate on real work in the classroom. As the control of schools has become less centralised, the length of playtime has reduced particularly over the lunch period to suit the needs of the administration of the school. The many changes in curriculum and alterations to admissions bringing younger children into school have also contributed to shorter playtimes. Play has been down-graded to at best a leisure activity rather than a crucial part of child development.

Loss of play outdoors

Alongside this pedagogical change people tend to walk less with greater use of buggies, and car travel reducing the amount of real exercise and contact with the community. From 2000 onwards studies start to show that active play and learning outdoors has deteriorated in many situations and young children are required to sit down for longer periods in order to be taught from an adult-controlled curriculum. Research has shown that children become less attentive as they are forced to sit down more following adult-directed tasks (Pelligrini and Smith 1998). Children are required to sit down more because of perceived demands from curricular changes rather than teachers focusing upon their developmental needs.

The National Trust further added to this debate in March 2012 in a report by Stephen Moss entitled 'Natural childhood'. The report demonstrates the dramatic decline in children's relationships with the outdoors whilst stressing the benefits of keeping them fit, learning about the world around them and having fun by building a den, picking flowers and climbing trees. The statistics reveal dramatic changes in just one generation:

- Fewer than 10 per cent of children play in wild places – down from 50 per cent a generation (30 years) ago.
- The roaming radius for children has declined by 90 per cent in one generation.
- Three times as many children are taken to hospital each year after falling out of bed, as from falling out of trees.
- A 2008 study showed that half of all children had been stopped from climbing trees, 20 per cent had been banned from playing conkers or games of tag.

Moss (2012)

So what has caused this? Is this linked to changes within our society about perceived risk?

Risk-averse culture

Recent years have seen the growth of a risk-averse society which appears to want to wrap children in cotton wool in order to somehow protect them from themselves and unseen dangers. However, as Douglas (1992) argues, the word 'risk' equates to 'danger' for many professionals. When considered within the present climate of litigation this can result in an avoidance culture because many practitioners genuinely fear for their own legal safety.

Various facts and misconceptions help to support the barrier to a balanced approach to risk. These are ably described by Tim Gill in his paper for the English Outdoor Council 'Nothing ventured: balancing risks and benefits in the outdoors' (2010: 3):

1   The number of school visits is in serious decline.
2   Visits and outdoor activities are excessively dangerous.
3   Teachers face a serious risk of prosecution.
4   Litigation is rampant.
5   The courts are systematically making bad judgements.
6   Some unions are advising teachers/support staff not to lead or take part in educational visits.

Increasing urbanisation

Many adults fear we are losing touch with nature as urban sprawl, traffic growth, rising crime figures, 'stranger danger' and reduction in the number of playing fields all add to a loss of freedom to roam, increased stress and obesity and reduced freedom of choice. Playgrounds have also become infected by risk aversion although in reality they are comparatively safe and fatalities are very rare. The 'zero risk option' has unintended consequences where playground re-surfacing with soft surfaces has led to expenditure of over £300 million in order to save three or four lives in the last decade. By comparison, basic traffic calming measures would have saved 30 to 40 lives. Soft surfaces are also part of the 'keep clean' culture which exists particularly in cities and big towns and avoids sensory engagement with natural materials.

Marketisation of childhood

The increased marketisation of children, electronic distractions and increasing screen time are also taking their toll. Society itself creates boundaries to children's learning – the ease of occupying a young child with an interesting electronic screen on a damp day for a busy parent who has work or household tasks to be done set against a walk in the park clearly creates difficult dilemmas. Children are more exposed to marketing and the incipient pester power which then results when next shopping. Shopping in itself has become for some families a joint activity or hobby which is done together, leading to some children wearing designer clothes which are expensive and therefore must be protected from dirt and damage. Children's clothes, books, toys and even food are used to sell products. Just consider how many cleaning products use images of young children – another aspect of the 'keep clean' culture.

The electronic information stream is not all negative and in some cases may actually provide good models of child rearing but it has also raised parental awareness of many potential hazards to their children from strangers, traffic, poor weather and other previously less visible perils and menaces. Furedi (2002) writes of the unprecedented rise in anxiety for children's safety through a 'culture of fear' which has harmed parental attitudes to children's safety outside and when they are unsupervised.

The effect upon practitioners

So how do these concerns relate to play and learning in the early years today? Most people agree that young children need time and space to run around, make lots of noise, let off steam, have permission to get dirty and learn about the world, but this is set against the real worry for their safety and possible litigious results. It also appears to be at odds with those who view learning as only achievable in formal settings. For practitioners there is a resulting minefield to cross involving reading guidance, following rules, satisfying requirements for first aid and other welfare regulations, policies, gaining permission from parents and form filling just to set foot outside the classroom door, let alone outside the setting. It is not surprising then that despite so much shared research about the value of playing outdoors some practitioners still opt out of daily outside experience for young children if the weather is not 'reasonable'.

New beginnings?

In contrast, Lindon (1999) and Gill (2006) emphasise that children have never been so safe. Tragedies involving young children can force adults to feel emotionally overwhelmed and helpless, leading to a rejection of any opportunities for risk, challenge and adventure. We all feel the horror of 'What if that was my child?' However, if we only see the world as a series of potential life threatening situations we would always take the zero option and deprive children of real life opportunities and freedom as they grow and develop. Somehow we have to set aside such paralysing fear and have a longer term view that outdoor play with risk, challenge and adventure is the best kind of child rearing we can provide. As Tim Gill states, 'Far from being a negligent or irresponsible act, giving children a taste of freedom is a crucial part of every parent's role.' Many parents already recognise and are increasingly vocal in untying the apron strings as recent challenges from the 'Playing Out' campaign in Bristol to create residential play streets, and the parents of two London children a couple of years ago who fought for the rights of their 5- and 8-year-old children to cycle to school illustrate, a move to nurture children to grow up wisely rather than as paranoid individuals who are fearful of leaving home.

Children are good at reading the value adults place on play and learning in different places. The adults are also often perceived as monitors who supervise rather than engage in play as Professor Iram Siraj-Blatchford (2001) found. Outdoors remains one of the few places where children can play independently, negotiate physically and socially on their terms as part of the learning essential to navigate through later life. The reduction of children's opportunities to access the benefits of physical activity, build their confidence, self-esteem and relieve stress are recognised by the National Playing Fields Association's research in 2000.

From 2000 onwards, studies start to show that active play and learning outside has deteriorated. This was highlighted by Sally Goddard Blythe (2000) 'The most advanced form of movement is the ability to sit still'. Likewise Goswami (2004) produced research which linked movement to babies' and young children's brain development. This crucial body/brain link ties in with the work of Vygotsky (1978) who stressed focusing on what children can nearly do in their emerging skills and 'use risk-taking to encourage them to push themselves further and extend their limit.' This links to Carol Dweck (2000) who introduces the idea of 'mastery' by using an 'I can do it attitude' rather than 'learned helplessness' as an essential key to learning which practitioners should consider carefully both in terms of school/setting ethos and in how they grow parental support for outdoor play and learning.

Child psychologist Aric Sigman (2007) stresses the benefits of what he describes as the 'countryside effect'. In his research he found that children who were exposed to nature scored higher on concentration and self-discipline; they also improved in reading, writing, maths, science and social studies; were better at working in teams and overall showed improved behaviour. Significantly they all didn't just learn better but they learnt differently with improvements in cognitive, affective, social/interpersonal and physical/behavioural areas.

National influences

Different sources of interest in the last couple of years reveal there are real grounds for optimism about the value our society places upon adventure, risk and challenge as well as playing outdoors. In the 'Sowing the seeds' report carried out for the Mayor of London (London Sustainable Development Commission 2011) it was stated that one in three children under 12 in London is missing out on a vital part of their development because they only experience six visits to a natural place in a year. The report argues that this experience should be part of everyday life for children.

Concerns about inequality in the UK in terms of access to outdoor play and learning opportunities were also seen as an important consideration in terms of access to outdoor, sporting and creative activities in the IPSOS MORI Social Research Institute survey (2011), researching the wellbeing of children living in the UK, Sweden and Spain. Family time spent doing things together was clearly woven into the fabric of everyday life in Sweden and Spain but was far less apparent in the UK. This was particularly true as children reached secondary education age. In the UK, stimulating outdoor activities for children from less well-off families in particular, dwindled alongside wellbeing whilst materialism increased.

Recent research by the Royal Horticultural Society revealed that more than 8 in 10 (81.6 per cent) of parents garden with their children aged 4–11 (poll reported in *London Evening Standard* 19 August 2014). However, almost half the parents questioned (48 per cent) said that their child knows more or the same amount about gardening as they do since less than 1 per cent (0.6 per cent) of parents were taught to garden at school themselves. Interestingly 58.8 per cent said their child now has access to a school garden, with 76.2 per cent revealing their youngster uses the facility. This does, however, sit alongside research by Savlon and Play England (2012) who found that 42 per cent of children aged 6–15 years had never made a daisy chain and 25 per cent had never rolled down a hill. A third had never built a den and only 10 per cent walked to school alone.

In the spring of 2012 the National Trust published a booklet entitled *50 Things to do Before You're 11 and Three Quarters*. It is a practical booklet which children (and parents) can engage in and record the achievement of 50 different challenges as adventurers, discoverers, rangers, trackers, and explorers. This shows a resurgence of interest in outdoor activities alongside other 'back to basics' moves in our society. The activities also link to a website: www.nationaltrust.org.uk/50things, so each child can earn a medal.

Adventurous outdoor play in other parts of the world

We can learn a lot from other cultures and comparative risk. Around the world, different cultural views as to the types of environments and attitudes to risk, challenge and adventure are very evident. Many of these are highly influential and positive for young children.

Forest Schools

The forest schools established in Denmark and other Scandinavian countries were first developed for children under 7 years to encourage positive experiences, skills development and participation outdoors in order to learn to respect the world around them and understand how their actions affect the environment. This was a parallel development to a school system based upon strong principles of citizenship and parental involvement, which were established to create 'meaningful education' within a democratic society based upon principles of child development, child wellbeing, and children's rights. Danish kindergartens are remarkable in the amount of freedom given to children as well as the high levels of risk they can undertake.

The Forest School movement has also had a growing impact on English schools and settings as research has demonstrated the personal, social and emotional benefits to children who are less confident or who have behavioural difficulties. I have experienced the work at Bridgewater Early Excellence Centre and Oxfordshire Forest Schools, as well as the ongoing link between Holland Park Ecology Centre and Chelsea Open Air.

Research about learning to manage risk and adventure in Forest School settings has shown huge value in the growth of personality with a range of learning traits showing improvement such as perseverance, concentration, motivation, and of course, skills. O'Brien and Murray (2007) alongside the research of Lucas and Claxton (2010) provide evidence of the improvement of the child's disposition to learn by being outside. In Norway, one in ten kindergartens are outdoors for at least three days a week for most of the year whilst there are enough hours of daylight. Lunch and rest time are enjoyed in a canvas tepee. The temperature is often low but the only real danger is wind chill so a reliable thermometer is observed regularly. The Norwegians state that as teachers they must be creative with the weather and use the environment to support each child's holistic development and resilience. Walking over uneven ground develops balance and co-ordination for 5 year olds climbing a 470 metre high peak for 3 hours with no toilet or home comforts – just what they can carry to cook on the fire for food stops.

We have begun to understand through the Forest School movement that risk–benefit analysis shows what the benefits of activities really are alongside the hazards, giving us the opportunity to see which are of the greatest value.

The New Zealand way

The Te Whariki approach in New Zealand aims for children 'to grow up as competent learners and communicators, healthy in mind, body and spirit; secure in their sense of belonging and in the knowledge that they make a valued contribution to society' (Ministry of Education 1996: 9). Risk and challenge is very evident in New Zealand settings alongside a strong ethos of belonging and communicating in terms of family and community relationships, empowerment and holistic development through exploration.

Reggio Emilia, Italy

The mothers who stood up to the Fascists in Reggio Emilia, northern Italy after the Second World War, established new nurseries where the creative, competent child is central to the philosophy to this day. The nurseries established the importance of the social relationships for each child which help him/her create knowledge and to research in multiple ways whilst exploring learning via 'one hundred languages' with no planned formal curricula or outcomes. The effects of this child-led philosophy are very evident in the beautiful indoor environments in the nurseries of Reggio Emilia today which are provided to nurture higher-level thinking. The Italians believe that the environment is a crucial strand in the interaction with the child and hence it is described as the 'third teacher'.

I remember watching 3 year olds using Stanley knives in the Diana Nursery of Reggio Emilia with great competence. I was fascinated but many colleagues were horrified. Later, in another Reggio, I observed a crawling baby poking its head into a round glass goldfish bowl with water with inhabitant goldfish without any staff over reacting, just calmly observing and taking note of the child's real interest and engagement. Certainly no one had written a risk assessment in either case. I began to realise how health and safety varies with culture in schools and settings.

Cultural aspects of play provision

In Europe, play streets and exciting public play areas with water, sand and real climbing and scrambling challenges are the norm not only in areas of housing but also in town and city shopping areas.

Cultural differences are very evident when children start in nursery. Despite having been shown around Chelsea Open Air and the practice of free-flow play and learning indoors and out throughout the year having been explained in detail, at the first sign of frost, very heavy rain or when their child has a slight cold, certain children are either kept at home or parents request they stay indoors. In these instances they are politely reminded that if their child is ill they should be at home but if not their access to indoor and outdoor play cannot be curtailed. Equally, we have children who arrive during the colder days of winter in so many layers of thermals that they generally do not get to the toilet in time. Children from cultures such as Scandinavia and many of the developing worlds, where outdoor play is culturally valued, are more attuned to responding to outdoor learning.

The Early Years Foundation Stage Curriculum

Our own Early Years Foundation Stage (EYFS) framework highlighted the importance of outdoor play alongside the indoors in the original 2008 version in commitment 3.3 of Enabling Environments: 'A rich and varied environment supports children's learning and development. It gives them the confidence to explore and learn in secure and safe, yet challenging, indoor and outdoor spaces.' In a revised version (2012) in item 3.57 of the Safeguarding and Welfare Requirements it states: 'Providers must provide access to an outdoor play area or, if that is not possible, ensure that outdoor activities are planned and taken on a daily basis (unless circumstances make this inappropriate, for example unsafe weather conditions)'. This is not an opt-out clause but a real opportunity for practitioners who have less on-site outdoor provision or reduced staff to be more creative. This may involve some careful planning in order to ensure ratios but there is no reason why as a group the children cannot go to a local park on a frequent basis if the assistance of CRB (Criminal Records Bureau) checked parents, trustees, governors and volunteers are enlisted. Whilst this may not be feasible on a daily basis, it can be achieved regularly for longer periods of time if resourced properly.

The outdoor provision suggested within the Early Years Foundation Stage (2008) theme of Enabling Environments emphasised the value of play both inside and out using a variety of real objects and tools to help young children develop key skills. This removes most of the risk as Montessori (1912) showed in her use of china during mealtimes, knives to cut up fruit, use of needles for sewing and carpentry tools so long ago. In the Statutory Framework for the Early Years Foundation Stage (2008: 33–36) a specific legal requirement for an annual risk assessment was stressed for the 'outdoor and indoor spaces, furniture, equipment, toys which must be safe and suitable for their purpose.' This is changed within the guidance for staff in the Revised Early Years Foundation Stage (2012) where within the Safeguarding and Welfare Requirements item 3.63 it is stated: 'Providers must have a clear and well-understood policy (for risk assessment), and procedures, for assessing any risks to children's safety, and review risk assessments regularly.' Later in 3.63 it states: 'Risk assessments should identify aspects of the environment that need to be checked on a regular basis, when and by whom those aspects will be checked, and how the risk will be removed or minimised.' Hence, the onus is now on the leadership and management of the setting or school.

Crucial support for outdoor learning is provided by Dame Clare Tickell's review of the EYFS (July 2011) and the resulting revised EYFS in March 2012 stressed the need for a greater focus on Physical Development including health by making it a prime area for learning alongside Personal, Social and Emotional Development and Communication and Language. Tickell also commented on the importance of the daily provision of outdoor play:

- Being outside and playing has a positive impact upon children's development and wellbeing.
- Being outside for first-hand encounters with the weather, the changing seasons and the natural world in all its richness and variety.
- Exploring what outside offers in terms of different opportunities, freedom, sensory exploration, physical activity and pure energy and enthusiasm.

The revised Early Years Foundation stage gives us a genuine opportunity to build firmly upon the underlining principles of the unique child, enabling environments and positive relationships using the characteristics of teaching and learning to create real experiences for young children to play adventurously, rise to appropriate challenges and take reasonable risks. This is particularly true in the prime areas and as children develop their play and learning opportunities at developmentally appropriate levels. These can be enhanced through building exciting connections through the specific curriculum areas.

Finally, a parent showed me a fascinating link to Geever Tulley (2007) on the Internet: www.ted.com/talks/gever_tulley_on_5_dangerous_things_for_kids.html. Tulley can be seen discussing the five dangerous things he feels parents should let their children do. These were:

- play with fire;
- own a pocket knife;
- throw a spear;
- deconstruct appliances;
- break the Digital Copyright Act.

Whilst some of these activities are questionable in terms of our youngest children and most of the video clips appeared to be primary children, it is his view that children learn so much more from these really adventurous experiences than when they are only given options he described as 'Dora the Explorer' experiences. Making and using real things such as a fire to cook on leads directly to discoveries about the basic science of combustion, intake and exhaust. Watching Tulley's video of children doing all these adventurous things is fascinating. Personally, I draw the line at sitting a child on an adult's lap to drive

Attitudes towards risk, challenge and adventure

a vehicle on private land which Geever describes as 'empowering' but I have witnessed such activity in several European countries and I recognise the similarity to 'the fascination that children have with all very big and powerful things like dinosaurs!'.

Conclusion

Practitioners have to make up their own minds as to their philosophy regarding outdoor play and risk-taking but careful discussion of Helen Tovey's (2007) view can help grow confidence and practical pedagogy. She states: 'Bumps, bruises, tumbles and falls are part of learning and we must not succumb to overwhelming anxiety or recklessness.' This balanced view provides a starting point for settings and schools to consider the body of research alongside their practice and work with parents to ensure young children have those essential and often awe inspiring experiences which they will never forget and which will enhance their holistic learning. Risk-taking is non-negotiable and something we must encourage and develop for the good of future societies.

CHAPTER 4

The benefits of risk, challenge and adventure

Introduction

There are major benefits of young children playing and learning outdoors. Whilst naturally supportive of child development, risk, challenge and adventure can, if appropriately provided, extend the horizons for all sorts of children whatever their background or ability. This chapter will examine how risk, challenge and adventure can impact on all areas of children's lives. It starts by looking at aspects of movement and child development. This leads on to a discussion about physicality as well as mental health and wellbeing particularly in relation to engaging with nature. Finally the chapter has a focus on inclusion by considering children with special educational needs and disabilities alongside gender especially in terms of the varied benefits for boys and girls. This chapter is about providing all young children with the opportunities to develop positively.

Movement and child development

> Children want space at all ages, but from the ages of 1–7, space, that is ample space, is almost as much wanted as food and air. To move, to run, to find things out by new movement, to feel one's life in every limb, that is the life of early childhood.
>
> Margaret McMillan (1919)

This comment from McMillan still holds true today. For many young children, on entry to a setting providing high quality nursery education and care, it is the space in the garden/outside area and all it has on offer in terms of movement, which equates with their sheer joy of being! The garden gives children the chance to be able to run freely, ride bikes, throw balls, make sandcastles and mud pies, create dens and hidey holes to name a few possibilities – it is in fact life changing.

Movement is probably the most important type of learning for young children. Isaacs (1952: 74) points out 'Words are at first merely a way of pointing to things, and but empty sounds until the children have had a rich contact with the things themselves, and explored them with hand and eye.' She goes on to stress that they start to understand concepts such as near and far, and up and down, by stretching, walking, running and jumping as their development advances. This hands-on physical experience in different scales gives young children real and tangible interaction with space, natural resources and the

The benefits of risk, challenge and adventure

environment. To them it is fresh and new as well as full of wonder, possible fear and excitement. This often leads to sheer ecstasy in being able to run, climb, hide, walk, dig, build, experiment, make and discover in a freer space than is available indoors. Often the outdoors provides opportunities too for children to 'test' their physical movement skills as is often seen when they swing from a branch or create a sand castle or mud pie. This develops self-confidence, self-regulation and wellbeing. Outdoors has a different pace in that children are often far more in control of being able to move more quickly or be still if they choose to, following their own agendas whilst interacting with others or being alone. They can learn about the weather and seasons and how long plants can take to grow with great care and attention. Children can experience the world through their whole physical being by playing freely outdoors and feeling the world around them by learning to use a range of tools safely and effectively. These can be spades, trowels, and watering cans for gardening; saws, knives, cable cutters and matches (some with appropriate adult teaching and supervision); to whittle, build dens and create small fires.

Physical Development is also the area of learning that adults most easily plan and develop outside in the revised EYFS. Of course, the other two prime areas – Personal, Social and Emotional Development and Communication and Language – as well as the specific areas are also crucial. They should be there to allow all the characteristics of effective learning to emerge and develop alongside one another via expert nurturing. Characteristics such as finding out and exploring, persevering and choosing the way to do things are naturally underpinned by adventure, risk and challenge within a suitably challenging enabling environment through planned and purposeful opportunities and appropriate adult intervention which follows and extends children's interests. There are endless possibilities to explore found natural materials as well as rules and boundaries. Overall a child who has had ample and appropriate experience of physical risk, adventure and challenge will show good control and co-ordination in both small and larger movements. They will also be confident with a range of tools and equipment and use them safely and effectively. They will through experience have far greater understanding of good health and safety in terms of their own hygiene and wellbeing.

Therefore, outdoor play is essential for our children because:

- Natural environments are diverse and flexible and support a wide variety of play and learning.
- Predominantly children see outside as free from adult rules and therefore more open to their play and can use it more creatively.
- Playing outside offers many more possibilities – construction, manipulation, ways of moving, control, and body mastery. It can also offer a sense of awe and wonder, and stimulate creativity, symbolic play and imagination.
- Children have their own starting point outside so they can play immediately and be independent.
- Play outside is powerfully diverse and provides rich opportunities to support individual and group physical, mental and emotional health.
- Being outside provides real and meaningful opportunities to learn, to recall and discuss things and have fun!
- Children have a natural appetite for freedom and growing their boundaries!

Child development as a natural process

Child development is a natural process which uses the senses to link to the developing body as well as building connections with nature. The natural world does much to support children through its calming and restoring therapy and health benefits such as vitamin D and serotonin. It is full of amazing opportunities and things of interest which children are fascinated by and curious to discover more about. Just think about the opportunity to observe the iridescent wings of a butterfly as it settles on a leaf or being under falling autumn leaves as they flutter to the ground. This leads children to naturally engage and persist in following up their discoveries which in turn leads to cognitive gains alongside evident pleasure and satisfaction. Children naturally start to observe others and what they do which in turn helps them become ready to explore other possibilities and adventures. As they start to appreciate the natural environment they become aware of the patterns of life cycles and the complexity and detail in the world around them. They start to feel they can do things for themselves and have the ability to solve problems and make connections with others. Finally, in partnership with adults, they start to develop an awareness of caring and begin to understand about sustainability. A child who is caring for a seed or bulb for the first time will look at it several times each day and water it to try to ensure that it will grow and thrive. This gives the child resulting feelings that he/she can do something almost magical and nurtures their willingness to try other challenges. Ultimately this leads to far greater attachment, agency and stewardship in later life which was recognised as crucial in the RSPB's *State of Nature* Report (2013) and by the United Nations Decade of Education for Sustainable Development, 2005–2014 (UNESCO 2014).

As an individual, each child explores and develops the skills, knowledge and understanding through their own life experience, starting from the security of their family. It is a vital and delicate process that takes time and may be disrupted in the case of looked-after children and others who are vulnerable. Young children progress from rolling over, sitting, crawling, standing, to walking, and go on to move up and down steps and hills, kick, catch, slide, run, jump and climb. This range of movements also offers a sense of risk and 'scariness' in itself as children develop their personal sense of overcoming challenges. If you watch young children who have been kept indoors and are deprived of genuine free movement for a while they tend to overcompensate for lost time and thus literally explode outdoors and run around wildly often being less aware of hazards. Toddlers tend to learn to walk inside, but when they move outside they are challenged by uneven surfaces which are not flat or predictable so they slow naturally. Different surfaces may be slippery or more difficult to negotiate in wind, rain or snow. A gentle slope appears to a crawling baby like a mountain and stairs likewise to a new walker. For a 3 year old only familiar to a level urban home, a slope may lead them to run, lose control and tumble head-over-heels until they have learned how to negotiate such a slope with emerging skill and confidence. Thus the internal risk assessment process starts to work and support children to take on challenges that are appropriate to their unique development and skills.

By playing outside, children are offered the opportunity and sheer joy to be a lot noisier and at times quieter and calmer than indoors, for example when watching a caterpillar crawl across a leaf. These experiences, which to the child are full of challenge, support their development through risk and adventures whether it be jumping in muddy puddles, creating a fairy house with sticks, shells and stones or spraying other children and adults with the hose pipe! The benefits of such opportunities are essential for each and every child.

Freedom of play

Being outside enables children to move freely within different spaces, to find and move resources of their own free will, to change the pace and flow of their play without the constraints of being indoors. This lack of predetermination is essential as infants move from functional play to pretend play as young as 12 months old. Being outside gives them the freedom and space to be whatever they want to be. Such pretend play is natural and unpredictable so that naturally occurring resources such as leaves, stones and sticks may become food and tools within a game.

The variety of spaces and levels are also important to children in developmental terms. Children can get into spaces no adult could possibly squeeze into and they need the 'hands on' experience of exploring concepts such as height and depth whilst playing together with their peers. The richness and open-ended possibilities are boundless outside, as is learning involving physical development and movement. Every child needs to crawl on wet grass as well as dry grass too.

Outdoor play and learning offers a wide range of natural elements to discover the properties of water, sand, rocks, mud, trees and gardens which also invite open-ended challenges. A school that provides such real lessons in areas like water conservation and recycling is the Edible School Yard in California. It even has an area of garden for picking flowers and nibbling leaves so children can create their own rose petal perfume and potions. This ongoing observation and exploration process is more easily accessed and supported outdoors because of the evident variety in changes in the seasons and weather, as well as adult willingness to be more flexible and accommodate children's desires. This provides a rich opportunity to provide developmentally appropriate learning based upon what really interests the young child at their pace whilst nurturing their responsibilities and self-belief.

The importance of physicality

From the new-born baby onwards, children are ready to function physically within their environment because of their biological and physical needs. Jim Greenman, when writing about the physicality of babies and young children in *Caring Spaces, Learning Places* (1988) comments 'Their job is to develop and test all their equipment.' Children need freedom and a genuine sense of challenge in order to do this so we need to step back, let go of their hands and watch them grow in stature, skills and confidence.

Montessori also writes about the child's love of the environment, of objects within it and adults as resources. Think of how most babies enjoy being bounced upon an adult lap and as they grow bigger the joyous fun of rough and tumble play, musical bumps, tag and swinging upside down on a bar. Just consider the care and fascination that a baby demonstrates when exploring the exciting resources of a treasure basket. Dancing, running, household tasks, riding bikes and scooters can all help children's whole bodies develop and also be serious fun and pleasure. By considering the importance of the physical maturation processes and how we as adults can support them effectively, we can provide suitably adventurous outdoor play with plenty of freedom for children to try things out for themselves using a risk–benefit approach positively.

Much of the work of Sally Goddard Blythe (2005, 2011, 2012) from the Institute for Neuro-Physiological Psychology seems to suggest that many children are not attaining in school the results that would be expected of them due to poor co-ordination, balance and immature motor skills. By encouraging children to develop their physical competences and confidence via adventurous and challenging physical play, we can also enhance many aspects of cognitive, social and emotional development. These children are physically satisfied and composed; they make friends and interact naturally on their terms as well as emerging as self-confident individuals. The provision of physicality should build naturally upon the child's individual physical development process and be holistically entwined with their cognitive, social and emotional learning. Any child who develops an appropriate level of physical skill will also be enhancing their self-esteem and underpinning their ability to persevere as well as nurturing their feelings of wellbeing. Conversely a child who is struggling to develop and feel confident and competent in effective movement and physical skills will feel negative and less willing to participate. Physical play also gives children the chance to revisit and practice movement and other skills with reasonable safely as each child matures and develops.

Problem solving and collaborative learning

Children during their earliest days need specific opportunities and experiences which develop their ability to collaborate. Whilst they cannot always do this without adult

Figure 4.1 Developing gross motor skills.
Image taken from *The Power of Physical Play* © Siren Films Ltd (2014).

The benefits of risk, challenge and adventure

support, a culture which promotes risk, adventure and challenges will provide children with real opportunities to co-operate, to listen and speak, to negotiate, to assert themselves appropriately and therefore to learn to behave well within new and different environments. We know that there is a causal relationship between behaving well and thinking effectively. Whilst indoors (and in better weather outdoors too) story and group activities lead to lots of discussion and valuable learning; it is through block play, obstacle courses, apparatus use, ball games, parachute play etc. that children learn to respect uniqueness and differences as well as the very important desire to question. Den making and the creation of exciting large constructions are particularly good activities in which children nurture each other in collaboration as they transform everyday objects into whatever they want it to be. Natural experiences such as snow also provide excellent opportunities to collaborate, solve problems, ask questions and learn holistically together.

Early years provision in schools and settings should be places of questioning, where you must ask the question and the answer questions you. The indoors and outdoors should be seen as one continuous learning environment that in itself provides genuine problems which the children use and are guided to use in a range of ways depending upon their individual starting points. Such aspects of learning are central to the revised Early Years Foundation Stage curriculum alongside health and physicality.

There is potential for learning in even the tiniest outdoor space and likewise space for problem solving and collaboration. Creating a home for ladybirds who then write letters to the children can initiate and nurture a wide range of learning on a small scale which naturally supports a range of fine motor skills and learning about the creatures themselves. It might also emerge through the potential of a mud kitchen, through digging for buried treasure, running, spraying and sprinkling water from a hose or watering can, heuristic and creative play or by taking some of the inside resources out. Exploring concepts through direct personal experience alongside your peer group, say when lifting a log or a stone to hunt for mini-beasts, adds the chance of greater learning by reinforcing the experience through talk then and there and later perhaps through making books in small groups. Moments and feelings can be caught in photographs and video for follow up later allowing children to participate, think and watch undisturbed. This is particularly valuable if you wish to create emotional responses to places.

Woodwork: an example of risk-taking and challenging collaborative learning

Woodwork is an excellent example of a risky activity which can take place both indoors and out but which requires specific adult teaching if children are to safely gain the skills and understanding they need for using tools and wood both effectively and creatively for their own purposes. It is an active physical experience that can occur indoors or out. It is important as it offers young children the chance to use real tools which have a risk element attached to them.

Pete Moorhouse (www.woodworks.wordpress.com) describes in useful detail how working with wood at Filton Avenue Nursery School in Bristol emphasises what a very special activity it is to introduce to young children as it really engages their involvement for extended periods of time, often in excess of an hour. He describes how they first need to learn the skills and appear to feel a sense of responsibility when working with real tools. They then go on to experience problem solving, reasoning and mathematical skills linked to their purpose. Communication and language also extend through conversation using new vocabulary. Creative expression is enhanced alongside manipulative skills. He stresses how the first essential to deal with risk is to train staff to work safely with wood and to set a ratio of 1:3. He also suggests a viewing area when other children are keen to watch. Woodwork can help provide life skills and well as creative explorative play.

Children's wellbeing

The Early Years Foundation Stage curriculum recognises that the invaluable and lifelong characteristics of effective learning begin in a child's earliest years. As dispositions such as perseverance and tenacity are recognised as valuable, it is also logical that the opportunities and activities offered to young children should support and extend their intrinsic motivation and fully engage their passions and interests. This cannot be effectively or fully achieved indoors. The right to play outdoors and in all weathers is crucial, as Marjorie Ouvry (2005) stresses. She emphasises the importance of young children enjoying as much time outside as possible in order to engage and interact with the natural environment. Marjorie also explains that children will develop some of the benefits from such an involvement as defined by Laevers et al. (2005) in their study of the relationship between children's involvement and their wellbeing. Deep involvement occurs when children engage and concentrate at a deeper level of interest or 'flow'. This supports emotional health and self-esteem, further driving children's desire to explore, and extends competencies, life skills and engagement with others and society. Adults who recognise children's interests and levels of involvement and support them help them to extend their motivation and self-esteem. This helps to reduce tension and allow children to feel good about themselves in both mind and body.

Some children feel far less inhibited outdoors, whilst some prefer indoors and some are able to use both to great effect naturally. Many traveller children and some refugee children seem to prefer being outdoors as that has been part of their life experience at home and it is familiar and empowering. Some children are more able outside and demonstrate mature play and language not so evident indoors. Many who are reticent to look at books or write indoors will feel more secure in using them outside when linked to an area of interest, e.g. a garage role-play. Their concentration span (because of their deep interest and security) can then often extend to deep involvement as they are motivated, interested in the activity and comfortable within the space. Others are more imaginative and assertive as again they are comfortable in the environment which is more open-ended and under their control.

The importance and value of being outside and using the environment for physical purposes in terms of wellbeing, mental and physical health is now well recognised. As society has changed, opportunities of 'going out to play' have decreased, and this has

Figure 4.2 Deep involvement.
Image taken from *The Power of Physical Play* © Siren Films Ltd (2014).

led to restrictions in children's exposure to their natural world as well as real threats to their health and wellbeing. Pressure on land has led to the reduction of housing with gardens, and parkland and school playing fields have also suffered. Organisations such as the Flourish Programme, Save Childhood Movement and Love Outdoor Play, Play England and Growing Schools have built awareness that children are having far less access to reasonable outdoor play space. Initiatives such as Forest Schools and The Wild Network which is being developed by the National Trust have at their core a risk–benefit approach in order to swap screen time for wild time through simple but profound interaction with everyday nature throughout the year.

Mental health

Outside play is often seen as having greater effect on physical health rather than mental health. Children build their emotional wellbeing by developing resilience. This is important through the whole of life as it is linked to positive self-image, harmony and inner calm. A young child who learns early on in life that he or she can do things independently will be more likely to see themselves as capable and competent in later life.

The Mental Health Foundation (1999: 6) found the following contributed to enhanced positive mental health in young children:

- learning to enjoy solitude to be able to live quietly and enjoy peace;
- initiating, developing and sustaining mutually satisfying personal relationships;
- playing and learning;
- resolving problems and learning from setbacks.

Learning to be comfortable in your own company is becoming harder for adults as well as children but outside is more likely to provide the quieter spaces and hidey holes where a child can be alone relatively speaking. Adventurous play enables children to become 'emotionally literate' by taking risks, using their initiative, dealing with conflict and making friends to the extent that some may actually reduce the likelihood of mental conditions later in life.

The awareness and value of learning through risk has started to be recognised. A project started by the Young Foundation reported in the *Evening Standard* on 15 February 2012 is starting to train teachers in resilience skills because children have become 'too soft' and don't know how to cope with failure. This project uses risk, challenge and adventure to support children and young people to become more resilient. This will be beneficial when they are older as they will be better able to deal with failure and adversity.

As much of young children's time is spent indoors in man-made environments with bought toys and equipment, important aspects of learning and development are in danger of being missed, especially if children have limited contact with the outdoors. Much of this is about discovering things for oneself rather than being taught. There are also long-term effects as young children who are kept away from the natural world and are given the message that it is dirty, messy and dangerous will only ever see it as that and never wish to explore it for themselves as the research of Thompson et al. (2008: 132) illustrates. Whilst indoors can be a rich environment for young children's learning, outdoors allows for far greater exploration. There is no comparison in picking up wooden or plastic bricks indoors to stones outdoors in terms of the richness of learning opportunity and the potential to inspire interests. The bricks are clean and regular, whereas the underside of the stones may reveal all manner of excitement underneath, providing huge learning possibilities. Such multi-sensory opportunities encourage the positive mental dispositions and attachments that connect to the basic need to belong and become. Each child through their whole body and mind can develop a strong sense of personal identity alongside an appreciation for natural objects and a sense of awe and wonder at the diversity of nature

Physical health

Today many children do not undertake enough physical activity. They live increasingly sedentary lives with shrinking physical demands and eat too much sugar and fat. This lifestyle has led to increases in stored fat and medical problems with obesity and diabetes. Physical development can be promoted by a culture of challenge, adventure and risk. The other main benefit of physical play is that by running, climbing trees and generally exploring in all ways outdoors leads to natural exhaustion and better sleep.

Article 24 of the United Nations Convention on the Rights of the Child stresses the need for children to have the right to the highest level of health possible. There is increasing evidence that children's reduced access and uptake of outdoor play has been a causative factor in increasing obesity, as well as diseases such as coronary heart disease, high blood pressure, Type 2 diabetes, stress, anxiety and depression in increasingly younger and younger children as illustrated by Biddle and Biddle (1989). Therefore, it is

The benefits of risk, challenge and adventure

not surprising that overweight children become obese adults with chronic medical difficulties.

Playing outside is a rich base to encourage all sorts of healthy habits that are essential life skills. We want to grow children who are not fearful of life or the future which is constantly changing, so teaching them about potential hazards (however small) is essential. Children then become far more physically skilled and aware of what their bodies can do. Washing your hands properly is a useful skill before meals and after using the toilet which the EYFS expects children to understand. Children can also learn a great deal through washing hands after stroking a pet rabbit or playing in the mud kitchen, exemplifying the importance of good hand hygiene as well as cultivating the understanding that whilst pet animals are wonderful to touch and mud is great to play with and explore, eating with dirty hands is not positive. Children's physical health improves by being outside more through reduced spread of infection as they are away from over-heated, stuffy rooms.

In January 2009, the National Institute for Health and Care Excellence (NICE) published health guidance about promoting physical activity, active play and sport for pre-school and older children (NICE 2009). The research stressed the value of physical activity being important for children's health and wellbeing and in contributing to their physical, social, emotional and psychological development. The researchers stress the importance of fostering family enjoyment, active participation and competence to intrinsically motivate children and therefore sustain their physical activity levels rather than the need to understand and conform to rules or master complex skills. Play and other spontaneous activities are valued particularly as 'Children and young people need to take risks and challenge themselves when involved in physically active play, sports and other activities, so they can learn their own boundaries' (2009: 38).

In conclusion, the report goes on to make various recommendations such as:

- the need to gather valid and reliable measurement of physical activity;
- improving ways of increasing and sustaining children's physically active modes of travel such as the use of family cycle ways in parks and old railway lines;
- enhancing ways of increasing and sustaining different types of activity in different groups by age, culture, ethnicity, disability, geographical area etc.;
- looking at what encourages and prevents children from being active including particularly the relationship to their family's involvement.

When going on adventurous expeditions and responding to a variety of self- and adult-chosen challenges, children become more robust in dealing with all weathers and a range of appropriate footwear, clothing and sun cream. Their large and small muscle groups develop and they are far better at judging hazards accurately, resulting in fewer accidents and incidents. Overall access to risk, challenge and adventure grows children's confidence in themselves and as a group they are less 'frenetic' and able to concentrate for far longer periods of time because they are engrossed in self-chosen challenges which extend their deeper level learning and skills overall. Freedom of movement gives children the chance to learn about their position in space, so through chances to swirl, spin and bounce they develop first-hand experience of height, depth, weight and growth.

We also need to recognise the importance of family influence and socialisation on children developing their movement skills and physicality. Early years settings can involve families in physical activities both indoors and out to help improve physical health. This not only includes outdoor play and games but also by encouraging them to walk, run, jump, climb, dance or cycle at an event such as a 'Welly Walk' or special workshop.

Engaging with nature

Natural play has long been recognised as important for children. Children have always been connected to nature emotionally but often lose this when they become adults. Nature provides the venue for children's engagement with risk, challenge and adventure as seen in the Finnish Skogsmulle (Forest Schools) and the Rain or Shine Nurseries of Sweden. The Scandinavian way of life is built around 'friluftsliv', which is a deep-rooted connection and cultural expectation to the natural world. For example this can be seen in a sitting baby exploring the qualities of a collection of fir cones, sea shells and smooth pebbles to a child enjoying the discoveries of Forest School experiences. They are first and foremost physical engagements but lead to higher order thinking. The child's balance of the love and understanding of our natural world is also critically important for its future sustainability.

Extensive research shows that young children have a strong and deep-rooted sensitivity to the natural world and benefit from it in different ways. Grahn et al. (1997) and Fjortoft and Sageie (2000) demonstrated how children who play in natural environments showed more advanced motor fitness, including co-ordination, balance and agility, and they are sick less often (Grahn et al. 1997). Pyle (2002) showed that exposure to natural environments improved children's cognitive development by improving their awareness, reasoning and observational skills. Spending time in nature has been shown to reduce stress and benefit treatment of numerous health conditions Kahn and Kellert (2002). Consider also what Wells and Evans (2003) show in their research demonstrating that the greater the amount of nature exposure, the greater the benefits.

Other research shows apparent contact with the natural world enhances the development of wonder and imagination (Cobb 1977; Louv 1991; Wilson 1997). Moore (1996) showed how children who play in nature have more positive feelings about each other. Moore (1986) and Bixler et al. (2002) showed how natural environments stimulate social interaction between children too. This research has more recently been affirmed by the Scottish Nature Kindergartens (Warden 2010).

In Japan, there is a recognised health benefit of spending time in forests with the word 'shinrinyoku', which literally means 'forest bathing'. Other countries emphasise the importance of early childhood education having values and purpose which will grow people who will value and look after our world as seen in Iceland, Australia, Denmark and Norway. They want children to become socially responsible and show respect for the environment and cultivate these traits and skills through their curriculum.

There is an emerging picture coming from the Natural Childhood Network Project which points to the importance of catching children's interest in the outdoors before they are 12 years of age so they see the outside is a positive experience. There is a growing desire to connect children to their world and nature in order to build more caring and nurturing citizens who are environmentally aware and will be advocates of our economic and environmental future. Surprisingly this is being supported by the economic recession as families are more inclined to use the natural environment as it has little or no cost associated with it as Arla's 'Kids Closer to Nature' campaign (National Schools Partnership 2012) discovered. They found that 70 per cent of parents are finding it a cheap day out to visit parks, gardens and green spaces or have a budget day at the seaside.

Supporting every child

Inclusion of a diverse range of children and families is a great strength in the early years and it is often the children themselves who break down the fears and potential barriers which can limit involvement and true participation in play. Again the ethos of a benefit–risk culture appears to widen the range of children and families likely to be involved. Values and principles are important in the school setting as inclusion requires commitment, collaboration and problem solving if all children are to genuinely experience risk, challenge and adventure for themselves.

Children from very diverse backgrounds, if brought together, can learn about one another, learn about difference, similarity, roles, rules and responsibilities and become both agents and advocates for inclusion. Clearly it is not all plain sailing as some children will display aggression, call names, and exclude others who are different. Equally they can learn through the experience that there are other children who 'buddy up' with those who are less strong, less able to communicate or play physically. These children can become exemplary role models and leaders with responsibilities towards their peers. By using positive behaviour strategies such as the philosophy of catching children being good rather than telling them off for negative behaviours, adults celebrate strengths and nurture positive images. The same 'buddies' can therefore help to reduce social exclusion, aggression and victimisation by quickly and quietly asserting themselves as positive role models. This child-led inclusion can be achieved through teaching appropriate conflict resolution skills, assertiveness and judging when to obtain adult help to intervene if required. There is also some natural variance in buddies as some will find different challenges, e.g. stroking a pet or helping to build a fire not to their liking whilst others will excel at Makaton signing or using a balance beam to help a peer gain confidence.

Children who are disabled, ill or stressed may need extra support from buddies and adults through their play and particular activities in order to support their individual needs. Going outside for some of these children, for example those on the autistic spectrum, can also be beneficial in other ways due to new experiential stimuli and surfaces. It may be quieter and calmer as noise and low ceilings indoors can interfere with learning for some of these children. Children with speech development and hearing difficulties will need to be considered if your school or setting is close to a busy road, rail track or aircraft flight path.

Natural light energises and helps support concentration. Think how tranquil blue is, how green helps one feel secure and cared for whilst brown brings us back to earth. The early years garden has both energetic areas and areas that emanate stillness and allow children to experience a sense of calm and spirituality as well as observe and learn without direct engagement in play. Some children, such as those on the autistic spectrum, will need very specific support to develop their understanding of danger and will also need to be taught how to play alongside other children. A careful risk assessment of your garden whilst supervising the child's first exploratory visits will allow you to identify the possible danger areas such as heights, gates and resources. Once thought through, the risk assessment can then help you plan areas and experiences that the child will need specific teaching and support with.

For children with statements of special educational needs and disabilities, their very unique and individual needs are doubly important as they too experience the risk, challenge and adventure of being outside. These children can be 'over protected' by well-meaning carers and families who can actually further restrict their learning by trying the 'keep them safe' and limiting their independence and chance to learn. Intuitively many families appear to recognise outdoors as providing the right sort of challenging environment that will extend their child's ability to learn.

The outdoor environment appears to be recognised as an area of opportunity and experience with numerous open-ended outcomes which can be tailored to individual needs in a way that is not feasible at home. Whilst this may mean adapting activities and experiences, the flexibility outdoors is easier to adapt to children who bring different experiences, interests and competencies with them. This in turn adds further depth and value to the culture and ethos of risk, challenge and adventure. The outdoor environment should provide opportunities for all children to:

- develop and consolidate skills relevant to their stage of development and learning;
- have their entitlement to a varied, broad and balanced curriculum;
- have their individual interest and motivations fostered and needs met.

Children with disabilities may also be limited by their condition in terms of motivation and mobility as well as their ability to play socially and communicate their desires, interests and needs. These children need to be given manageable experiences appropriate to them in small steps. The next exciting opportunity should be to nourish and nurture latent ability that may never have been given the opportunity to surface before. Appropriate individual attention to each child and family along with respectful discussion to build trust will lead to the joint removal of potential barriers so that the child can enjoy and benefit from play indoors and out.

Inclusion case study

Over the years we have included a wide range of children with special needs and disabilities at Chelsea Open Air. Some children have been on our roll, whilst others often with severe disabilities have visited from local schools including the Chelsea Children's Hospital School. I have witnessed the outdoor environment work its own particular 'magic' in providing special and unique challenges for these children too. Such severely disabled children have benefitted from being in a much cooler and 'hands on' environment, as well as having the chance to be real children away from the stress and demands of their individual conditions within the hospital environment.

Other children with physical needs have benefitted from the challenge of different surfaces and obstacles to negotiate, touch and explore. Those with communication and speech difficulties are often inspired by what is on offer outside and thus are nurtured to move forward in their development too, often through singing to start with. However, some children on the autistic spectrum can find the space outside sometimes quite threatening but via clever planning can gradually take small steps to explore, and have some time outside little by little by building upon their particular interests. With time as they start to really explore, play and discover whilst of course carefully observed and supported, different and more challenging experiences can be added. Careful thought has to be given to each child's access and safety but where there is a 'can do' attitude from the staff and extending trust from the family, ways can always be found. As a rule always start from what each child can do and build upon their individual interests and widen opportunities to climb, slide, swing, hide, delve in sand, water and earth, grass or bushes, and to crawl along tunnels all provide different challenges for different children.

In C's case he arrived in nappies, with no speech, and bottom shuffling. He came from a professional family who were conversant in four languages and was the oldest of three. He had a statement of special educational need for a very rare genetic condition. He was motivated by being with his peers as he was a cheeky, social being and would move at speed to any garden door on entry to nursery in order to find his friends. Once outside he used low walls and objects to pull himself up and little by little began to walk. He was also supported in his toilet training as a first focus in order to include him as well as boosting his independence skills. He quickly mastered this and became a great observer and communicator using Makaton at speed alongside a cheerful grin to get his messages across. When he moved on to primary school I asked him what he would miss most. He responded in sign: 'the garden'.

For more able, gifted and talented children the garden is a haven of opportunity which can extend thinking, skills, experience and understanding in thousands of ways. Thus going on explorer hunts with special jackets and back packs, creating weather reports and videoing them, drawing and discussing local architecture, growing insectivorous plants, measuring dinosaur footprints or designing and making at the woodwork bench are the jumping off point for many who are advanced in certain aspects of their learning.

In R's case he was finding settling in challenging until his interest in architecture was discovered. Starting by an in-depth look at the school building which dated from 1587, we were able to 'fuel his fire' via photographs, paintings, books, and then we moved on to one-to-one expeditions to local places of interest including churches, Peter Jones restaurant to view the rooftop view of the area, and the Albert Bridge. One particular ancient Ladybird book of mine about church buildings became his most precious possession and at night was safely tucked under his pillow! It led to him reading, writing and drawing a wealth of local structures as well as creating his own in block play and via woodwork constructions.

It is a myth that children who are more able and those with disabilities and special needs have less need to experience risk. It is only by taking sensible and positive risks that they too will learn about the world and how they fit within it. We know children like and benefit from having boundaries but they all need to experience that tingling sense of excitement of 'flow' by overcoming physical and mental challenges by finding the right balance between keeping safe alongside exploring and making their own choices. For all the children, the garden and outdoor experience provides the rich basis of a real childhood with the opportunity to experience things on a different scale and in different ways. They can play with different children and have fun getting wet, dirty and in different dimensions which are simply not feasible indoors however relaxed one is. They experience awe and wonder with the changing seasons, weather and wildlife. They develop a vast array of life skills that will lead to future engineers, artists, scientists, writers, gardeners, carers etc.

Gender

In the nursery age group, evidence has shown that girls tend to be drawn to activities which involve adults, whilst boys tend to be drawn to activities such as construction, climbing and gross motor skills.

Research by Parkin (1997) and Walkerdine (1996) has shown that boys in particular are at risk of becoming disaffected as they do not take up the right 'positions in pedagogic discourses'. Some do not take part at all, often choosing to spend longer periods of time out-of-doors engaged in high levels of physical activity as they do not feel at home in the domestic imaginative situations chosen by girls. Payley (1984) also in her fascinating study of boys and girls in her classroom found that the curriculum she offered suited the girls better than the boys as the girls were more willing to tackle activities associated with 'work'. The boys would avoid these in favour of block play and vigorous imaginative role-play often associated with super heroes.

Research into visual motor integration from Yerkes (1982: 4) showed that children's behaviour indoors was different from that of children learning outdoors who became 'strikingly assertive and imaginative'. Hutt et al. (1989) found that boys spent more time than girls outdoors on physical play and girls spent more time outdoors on material play. Bates (1996) found that when the space indoors became overcrowded it had different effects on boys and girls with boys becoming more aggressive and forming groups whilst girls played alone and became more isolated. These different pieces of research should also be considered alongside research from Nobel et al. (2001) looking at gender and learning styles in relation to an education system which seems to place greater value on visual and auditory styles rather than kinaesthetic styles which boys seem to favour in their early years. From this research it would seem that:

- outdoor play affects children in different ways;
- we need to consider the balance of visual, auditory and kinaesthetic learning styles indoors and out;
- some children prefer to play outside whilst others prefer indoors;
- outdoors can give a different picture of a child's learning;
- playing outdoors may well give children the opportunity to be more assertive, creative and imaginative in different ways;
- overcrowding indoors can affect behaviour negatively.

A case study of gender play

At Chelsea Open Air, many of our boys generally find it easier to play outside. They are drawn to the space and physicality available outside. They appear to favour activities such as large construction, climbing, gross motor skills involving spatial skills and equipment such as bats, balls, bicycles, ladders, tools and den making resources. These seem to satisfy their desire for greater independence, thirst for practical tasks with a clear purpose, and often later linguistic development and self-esteem.

Some of the girls are more inclined to be 'fair weather' garden users and some avoid the inclement days if they can. Curiously they are often perceived as more conservative and benefit from the genuine opportunities to explore risk, challenge and adventure outside because they need the physical challenges in terms of movement, independence and raised self-esteem as well as the need to develop and extend their problem solving skills. They particularly loved a challenge based around the fairy story of Jack and the Beanstalk when we turned it around to create a new story when Jack's sister Jill climbed the beanstalk before him. This made the garden for this group of girls more 'girl friendly' by adapting it to their motivations, interests and needs.

Outdoor play and its inherent provision of adventure, risk and challenge for young children can help positive development in both genders. The boys gain the opportunity to use their strengths in an environment which is natural and encompasses their interests and is supportive of their needs. These then support the further development of their concentration, engagement and communication skills. Girls can benefit in different ways by using their strengths in language, relationships and collaboration to grow greater confidence and problem solving skills particularly in risk-taking, getting messy and stretching their boundaries.

Conclusion

There are many benefits of risk, challenge and adventure for all young children that are backed by a wide range of research from around the world. The outdoors not only supports children's holistic development and health, but also gives them the confidence and chance to explore and seek out further new dynamic experiences that will support them through life's many transitions.

CHAPTER 5

The role of the adult

Introduction

This chapter looks at the specific role of the adult. The role of the adult is complex and involves both legal and professional responsibilities, however, the main focus here is on supporting learning and development through risk and challenge. The chapter considers the qualities that are needed for the role and stresses the importance of being a good role model to build a climate of mutual trust with children, families and colleagues. It then looks at the main professional responsibilities in facilitating high quality outdoor play and learning and how practitioners can provide core experiences and opportunities which involve risk and challenge for all the children in their care.

Key skills and qualities

Practitioners need to have a range of different skills, abilities and professional understanding to fulfil their role effectively. These include:

- Professional skills such as meeting the EYFS educational, welfare and care requirements, promoting positive self-esteem and liaising with families. This underpins the whole role and is essential for the wellbeing and progress of all children as well as helping to ensure that parents are confident in you as a highly competent practitioner.
- Organisational skills such as designing and using long, medium and short term planning, providing accessible labelled storage and writing clear observations and reports. These strategic skills are crucial in that they allow the organisation inside and out to function effectively and efficiently for the benefit of all.
- Interpersonal skills such as establishing respect and trust with children and families as well as inspiring and motivating colleagues. These are fundamental as relationships and trust form the foundations for play, learning and high quality teaching and engagement.

Linked to these skills are certain qualities or characteristics that underpin the adventurous practitioner. The practitioner who is keen to develop risk, challenge and adventure within their setting is likely to display the following key qualities:

The role of the adult

Passion

This is probably the most important quality as it not only includes the practitioner's 'enthusiasm for children', which is a key attribute, but also the drive to make a difference and therefore it is not always an easy or comfortable role to play. This strong desire creates the true early years practitioner who is there first and foremost for the young child and their right to learn through adventure, risk and challenge.

Perseverance

This is linked to 'dedication' and 'tenacity'. It is about the ability to stand up for your beliefs about children's rights, needs and education as well as sometimes overcoming bureaucracy linked to risk and challenge. It is linked to passion in that it is the insistence, drive and determination to ensure the best for the young child inside and out.

Willingness to take risks

Sometimes the status quo needs to be shaken up in order to improve a child's outdoor play and learning. This quality may require a practitioner to research, think and plan, as well as negotiate with different parties about the essential need for risk, challenge and adventure being elements of each child's play. To do this, practitioners must have the readiness and preparedness to be risk-takers too.

Compromise and pragmatism

These are the other aspects of perseverance and willingness to take risks. These qualities allow practitioners to accept that small wins lead to gradual progress towards the final goal. Working as part of a team requires that practitioners co-operate and collaborate and, at times, compromise realistically to allow challenging play and learning to go on even if not in the most ideal fashion.

Patience

This is a hugely important quality in terms of dealing with 'the system'. Being able to endure in a fairly serene fashion far from ideal circumstances, manage your own anger, frustration and exasperation with your challenges will help you to understand these feelings in children and tolerate the variable capacity of colleagues and families to understand your passion for risk and challenge.

Flexibility

Practitioners need to be highly adaptable to children and adults who do unexpected things, to variable environments which are unpredictable due to weather conditions and to bureaucracy which can restrict budgets or alter legalities without consultation. Maximising the moment is a skill which can allow practitioners to make the most of an unexpected situation such as a bird flying into a room by capitalising on the huge learning potential that is suddenly presented.

Respect

Respect for people's various views and diversity is vital and can lead to a multiplicity of experiences being available within the setting/school for the children which improves the quality of their experiences and adventures. It is about appreciating and valuing the miscellany of backgrounds, views and ideas whilst weaving them into the high quality provision indoors and out.

Creativity

This is essential as practitioners may not have ideal premises or very limited space or resources. Being able to use resources in an original or different fashion and adapt to different learning characteristics is highly beneficial. As a whole team, practitioners often forget the untapped skill base they alone can provide. Colleagues within a team, if really collaborating, can be inventive, imaginative and inspirational to each other and with the children and families and provide highly creative challenges and adventures.

Genuineness

This is about being authentic, knowing yourself and what you stand for. Young children are great judges of character and are quick to sense if you really don't like being outside!

Love of learning

This underpins the whole role. In order to inspire young children, their families and colleagues, an adventurous practitioner must show their commitment to being a life-long learner. Practitioners need to develop a dynamic and outgoing manner. If, for example, you are scared of spiders, you should still be able to engage with and value one when a child brings it to you without actually touching it or displaying any fear and then maximise their learning through books, the Internet and by looking at other mini-beasts.

Stamina

This is about doing a very demanding job in a sustainable fashion at a high quality over time be it a day, a week or a year. Ensuring you spread your energy over each day, week and year is critical for the wellbeing of the children, your colleagues and most of all yourself.

The role of the adult

Sense of humour

Finally, learning needs to be fun. Children will love and respect you but if they can laugh with you when something is funny, even if the joke is on you!

A note of caution: these qualities or characteristics do involve personal perceptions and may be interpreted differently from different standpoints, for example that of a head teacher or a parent.

Helen Bilton in her book *Outdoor Play in the Early Years* (2002, xi, 105–6) illustrates many qualities clearly when she stresses the importance of staff attitudes to supporting children's engagement outdoors within a managed and cared for environment. She describes the adult role as 'keeping a watchful eye, observing, scanning, anticipating problems, knowing who may need help, but at the same time giving children a degree of privacy.' These personal 'antennae' give practitioners the instinctive wherewithal of what is happening outside even if they cannot see or hear it.

KEY RESPONSIBILITIES

This next section gives an overview of the main pedagogical aspects which are central to the role by looking at the responsibilities laid down in the EYFS.

Planning enjoyable and challenging learning

The Early Years Foundation Stage (Department for Education 2008) states that 'providing well-planned experiences based on children's spontaneous play, both indoors and outdoors, is an important way in which practitioners support young children to learn with enjoyment and challenge' and that through play children 'can take risks and make mistakes.'

The revised Early Years Foundation Stage (2012 1.9) further developed this by stating that 'each area of learning and development must be implemented through planned, purposeful play and through a mix of adult-led and child-initiated activities'. The foundations of this approach are exemplified within the Characteristics of Learning, which underpin the pedagogical provision for young children. The EYFS acknowledges that 'play is essential for children's development, building their confidence as they learn to explore, to think about problems, and relate to others.' The EYFS also stresses the importance for practitioners to plan for and provide a rich array of play and learning, which are enjoyable, adventurous and challenging. The Characteristics of Effective Learning strengthen the areas of learning for both prime and specific areas as they demonstrate to practitioners and families clearly how children should be learning in their setting/school.

Much of the terminology used in Table 5.1 also strengthens and reinforces many of the important messages of adventure, risk and challenge. This is particularly true of the ways in which children engage with people and their environments, e.g. playing and exploring and active learning. It is also evident in the uniqueness of each child in terms such as: being willing to have a go, having their own ideas and choosing ways to do things. These phrases/features appear to mirror many of the practitioner

Table 5.1 Characteristics of effective learning

Playing and Exploring *Engagement*	**Finding out and exploring** ● Showing curiosity about objects, events and people ● Using senses to explore the world around them ● Engaging in open-ended activities ● Showing particular interests
	Playing with what they know ● Pretending objects are things from their experience ● Representing their experiences in play ● Taking on a role in their play ● Acting out experiences with other people
	Being willing to 'have a go' ● Initiating activities ● Seeking challenge ● Showing a 'can do' attitude ● Taking a risk, engaging in new experiences, and learning by trial and error
Active Learning *Motivation*	**Being involved and concentrating** ● Maintaining focus on their activity for a period of time ● Showing high levels of energy, fascination ● Not easily distracted ● Paying attention to details
	Keeping on trying ● Persisting with activity when challenges occur ● Showing a belief that more effort or a different approach will pay off ● Bouncing back after difficulties
	Enjoying achieving what they set out to do ● Showing satisfaction in meeting their own goals ● Being proud of how they accomplished something – not just the end result ● Enjoying meeting challenges for their own sake rather than external rewards or praise
Creating and Thinking Critically *Thinking*	**Having their own ideas** ● Thinking of ideas ● Finding ways to solve problems ● Finding new ways to do things
	Making links ● Making links and noticing patterns in their experience ● Making predictions ● Testing their ideas ● Developing ideas of groupings, sequences, cause and effect
	Choosing ways to do things ● Planning, making decisions about how to approach a task, solve a problem and reach a goal ● Checking how well their activities are going ● Changing strategy as needed ● Reviewing how well the approach worked

qualities mentioned earlier in this chapter. So how can the practitioner use these characteristics?

The practitioner uses their knowledge of the children, their interests and needs as a starting point for providing, supporting and extending the characteristics of learning and their related domains of social and emotional development, physical development and cognitive development across the curricular provision. These characteristics are linked closely to the sequence of child development and the increasing complexity of learning and child self-regulation. Hence the practitioner's role is paramount. Playing and exploring within an environment based on active learning should provide the most secure, fulfilling and relevant experience for the young child. The prime areas of learning and development – personal, social and emotional development, physical development and communication and language – also include the most important aspects of these characteristics and those of lifelong learning in terms of relationships, physicality and communication.

Social and emotional development

A good starting point for the young child is the provision of broad and balanced experiences indoors and out offering first-hand exploration in different scales linked to their interests. Alongside this should be practitioners who engage and talk with children about their interests and provide the next steps for their development and learning. This may be as diverse as the necessary encouragement and a hand to hold if a child is lacking in confidence when starting to balance along a low wall to the challenge of problem solving independently when joining wires to a battery and bulb in order to create a simple electrical circuit. A wide range of open-ended experiences within the learning zones will provide a secure base for the child to explore, gain confidence and start to establish relationships at their own level. As a child's social and emotional development emerges and capacities such as trust, friendship, assertiveness, listening and speaking plus self confidence develop, the child will move from relying on practitioners to support and encourage their learning to self-managing their learning and gradually becoming autonomous and independent. Thus every interaction with practitioners and other children can be significant in terms of exploring how one becomes a social being. This may mean practitioners getting really involved by co-constructing and taking on a character role within imaginative play or standing back and observing whilst a child sorts out a conflict. It may also mean the practitioner scaffolding learning by feeding back the processes a child has used when problem solving to help them see what they could try next as well as hinting at other possibilities to take them further by altering the resources available for them.

Physical development

Physical play is the first type of play to emerge as young children have an inbuilt psychological drive to do things for themselves. This motivation is important as it helps them succeed as learners and in being able to self regulate. Once children have positive self-esteem and feel safe and loved, they feel comfortable about taking risks and exploring

Figure 5.1 Physical development.
Image taken from *The Power of Physical Play* © Siren Films Ltd (2014).

new challenges. Again the practitioner role in physical development may involve standing back and trusting a child to climb a tree safety without saying a word. It may also involve demonstrating through one-to-one teaching and then encouragement as a child uses a hacksaw successfully the first few times. Judging when to intervene or to stand back is as unique as each child but practitioners also need to consider their well intended words may break a child's concentration by using phrases such as 'Be careful!'

Communication and language

Babies and young children are born to communicate and the early interactions with family, friends and practitioners establish the foundations of satisfying relationships. All children benefit from the extended opportunities to talk outside. Motivation is again key outdoors as there is so much that interests children and thus stimulates their communication skills. The changing weather and seasons as well as the interactive nature of opportunities outdoors awakens the child's senses and inspires talk. Through sensitive observation and interaction, practitioners can pick up on children's interests, follow their engagement and really focus upon what they are doing. Outside is often a more comfortable venue for practitioners to engage children in discussion to develop both talking and listening skills about their play. The varied opportunities, larger scale and physical space can often lead to the shyest child finding their voice and confidence outside as well as being free to explore volume and pitch. Outside in the nursery garden may be the only place that some young children experience real peace and quiet in our hectic lives. Experience such as megaphones, tube telephones, and clipboards and pencils can underpin activities with real reasons to communicate and write in context through imaginative play, treasure trails, and mini-beast hunts. For literacy a range of

The role of the adult

outdoor books, both fiction and non-fiction, to read and use for research should be easily available in a cosy dry corner or den as well as resources for mark making on a large scale with decorating brushes and water or giant chalks; an office with relevant writing and recording resources; and a range of dance, music and imaginary play etc.

Through these and other activities plus careful planning, practitioners can provide resources which lend themselves to supporting and extending young children's communication, language and literacy.

Creating and thinking critically and the specific areas of learning

Problem solving alongside quality practitioner intervention and support is a process of reciprocal interaction. Children can develop deeper understanding via sustained shared thinking and engagement in varied cognitive challenges. The real skill of the practitioner is having a rich repertoire of adaptable pedagogical activities and experiences which they can draw on as appropriate to each child. This involves differentiating the curriculum to match the level of challenge required to meet different children's needs and extend them further within one activity by careful questioning and appropriateness of task. It also requires skill in balancing child- and adult-initiated activities to facilitate children learning in the numerous and inter-related skills, knowledge and understanding that underpin the specific areas of learning – literacy, mathematics, understanding the world, and expressive arts and design. This can be achieved, for example, through the daily professional provision of story reading with props that encourage children's concentration, understanding and involvement to then acting out stories on a smaller or larger scale outside in order to create the environment and actions that the story involves. It may mean practical provision and explanation like using giant egg timers to ensure equitable access to precious or limited resources such as a visiting animal or the bicycles. This also then helps to explain the passage of time mathematically as well as turn taking and therefore becomes cross-curricular. It can also start from visiting a gallery or museum on an expedition and then returning to use clay and other raw materials in an open-ended fashion to create portraits or masks, giving the children very wide creative parameters.

Observing and recording children's learning and progress

What is observation?

The cycle of observing, planning and evaluating is well established in the early years but it is important to consider what these terms mean and the principles which underpin and strengthen them in relation to risk, challenge and adventure. Observation is a normal starting point and is part of daily quality practice for practitioners. It is about a unique child in self-chosen activity as well as adult-led activities. Good observations should demonstrate what a child can do, where they are learning and why it is significant for that individual. Observations therefore need analysis to identify and assess the achievement(s) and decide upon the child's next steps. The involvement of parent and children's contributions is also important.

Why observe?

Practitioners need to cultivate a full and rounded picture of each child and their achievements via a variety of observations. A range of observations is also required in order to make a summative assessment of the child's progress for the Foundation Stage Profile in the reception class. Different types of observation provide different kinds of evidence. They can be supported by a photograph, a sample of writing or drawing, a recording of a conversation, or DVD material of say a construction, model or creation. Each observation should help practitioners to plan more accurately for the individual child and for groups of children. In terms of planning some of the implications might be:

- What do we need to change, extend or develop to build and/or challenge this child's interests, needs, development, skills, knowledge and understanding indoors and out?
- How can we ensure that this child and others access the learning opportunities provided through challenging play indoor and out?

Types of observation

- Participant observations. These are when practitioners are fully involved working with children as they observe them.
- Planned participant observations. These take place during an adult-led activity, which will have specific learning intentions.
- Large group observations. These are useful as they provide practitioners with the opportunity to observe how a child responds within a larger group in terms their involvement, interests, concentration and responses.
- Incidental observations. These are the things you notice in passing and are often recorded quickly on sticky labels or 'Post-it' notes.
- Informal conversations. These record the language and communication skills of both the verbally confident child and those new to English or those who are at the earlier stages of speech development.
- Samples of evidence. These are many and varied and include drawings, mark making, emergent writing, art and craft, construction and models plus photographic and DVD recordings of types of play, dance, music and movement. They are often easily gathered using a digital camera outdoors providing a permanent record.

Planned focus observations are many and varied. They include:

- five-minute continuous observation during self-chosen play;
- tracking observations across a session to look at choices and patterns;
- areas of learning observation allow practitioners to look at the use of particular provision, resources, types of play and access by different groups.

Adapting planning and provision using assessment and evaluation

Having gathered together a range of evidence, practitioners need to consider each child's skills, knowledge, understanding, dispositions, attitudes and characteristics of learning. This is an assessment, which allows them to evaluate and adapt core provision to take each child forward in their learning and development. Having seen their achievements and progress over a period of time, practitioners need to summarise this as a more formal assessment before reflecting as to what their next areas of development should be and the types of activities, experiences and opportunities they will need to move onto. This need not be complex but can draw together the daily and weekly assessment conclusions of the staff team into longer term aims and systems which then feed back into the next phase of planning as PLODS (possible lines of development). This may result in specific teaching activities, new and different opportunities and challenges or one-to-one support in both indoor and outdoor environments. For example, a child who has developed their physical skills and prowess in balancing on planks, ladders, beams and stepping stones at low levels would be likely to benefit from an experience like weaving poles to challenge them to use their body in a different plane or manner. This could also lead to the child designing and creating a climbing structure in order to challenge themselves further.

How does this feed into planning?

Experienced practitioners use planning to provide structure and co-ordination of a range of stimulating developmentally appropriate activities and core experiences, which can be differentiated to the unique interests and needs of all the children within the indoor and outdoor zones. For example, if a practitioner plans an adventurous expedition for a few children who are interested in bridges, the practitioner could on their return initiate a bridge building experience using books and photos of different bridges for group discussion purposes. This could lead into co-constructing a bridge with resources such as blocks, crates and planks which could act as a catalyst towards the children's next step of drawing designs for their own bridges.

The practitioners decide upon overall learning intentions for the period. For example, during new children's induction phases lots of access to experiences which are familiar from home or previous settings will allow them to feel comfortable as they get used to many new children and adults and start to build relationships. Later on in the year there may be a particular group of skills or behaviours which the team have identified as being in need of further development. This can be a practical activity such as putting on and taking off clothing and footwear in role-play areas or more specific teaching such as using pencils to draw mini-beasts found outside whilst looking down a magnifier. At other times the planning may focus on say a festival or event, a visitor or special experience such as a farm visit or possibly an expedition out into the local community. Such experiences are often used to add richness and breadth as well as gradual extension and challenge to core provision and adult-led activities. An example could be the Chinese New Year where the children have helped set up a restaurant in the role-play area indoors and are exploring Chinese symbols in the graphics area with Chinese pens. Meanwhile outside they are learning Chinese dancing with ribbon sticks led by a Chinese parent or visitor whom the practitioners have invited in to share their expertise.

Learning Outside the Classroom (www.lotc.org.uk) in partnership with Learning Through Landscapes (www.ltl.org.uk) have produced some helpful cards to support practitioners providing ideas for communication and language plus literacy and understanding the world including mathematics out of doors in the early years. These are linked to actual case studies and give practical activity ideas. The ideas include a visit to a theatre linked to a traditional tale, using natural materials for discovery-based learning, creating a market stall, mini-beast homes, ice art, play dough printing and leaf counting.

Evaluating planning

Planning needs frequent consideration by the staff team if it is to adapt to the needs of the children daily, weekly, fortnightly, termly and annually. This allows for changes to be made and new ideas and developments to be incorporated for both individuals and groups through observation. Any gaps or identified changes to play and learning can also be implemented to ensure full curriculum coverage.

'Grabbing the moment' in terms of provision is important too. Increasingly we are moving towards greater structure in the curricular education of young children as they go into formal schooling earlier and earlier. However, the revised Early Years Foundation Stage (2012) is still based in high quality play and in many situations the practitioner is a non-participant in this play. This is particularly true outdoors and practitioners are better able to observe very closely and intervene if relevant. It is crucial to use any rich opportunities when the 'teachable moment' arises.

> On a very cold winter's day when passing a down pipe which was pushing out steam from the hot water which was going into the drain, a child remarked 'Oh look! It's smoking.' So the practitioner discussed what might be happening and whether or not the pipe was really on fire. It led to a large amount of scientific investigation.

See Appendix 1 for examples of planning.

Organising and resourcing learning opportunities

Practitioners should carefully consider how they can design activities and opportunities within the zones to maximise challenging and adventurous play and learning. This may be as simple as adding a new resource every day or by extending the opportunities in construction play. This could be achieved by using tape or string instead of the connecting pieces in Mobilo to make it far more challenging. Despite the unpredictability of the weather and the changes in our seasons, skilful use of long, medium and short term planning alongside creative use of effective resources and equipment can be established to create loose plans for the year and certain activities for particular weathers.

The role of the adult

Whilst there are catalogues full of the most amazing resources, in an ideal world the actual play area/garden should provide the catalyst for high quality play without any additions. However, for the practitioners there are core resources which are very useful if collected beforehand. The provision of weather boxes, festival and celebration boxes plus role-play boxes such as the garage, the castle, pirates, the garden centre, the market stall, the building site and ice cream stand all bring a wide range of relevant resources to extend children's learning. This is also the case for small role-play such as the farm, space station and dolls' houses. For example, setting up the space to create a car wash with the bikes to improve both gross and fine motor skills as well as co-ordination or running horse races using giant egg timers pretending the bikes are horses provides fun and physical challenge as well as aspects of mathematical development. When establishing a garage outdoors the use of the big blocks to create the structure, clipboards and pens, nuts, bolts, cardboard blanks for number plates, car manuals, tools, tyres, buckets and sponges with the bikes as a car wash will draw many children in and allow them to design, build, collaborate, engineer, write, record and communicate in a variety of ways. Specific learning intentions can be carefully established by the practitioners to draw out the required skills and dispositions for individuals within the activities.

Providing age and developmental stage appropriate experiences for children

Free-flow play is recognised as a way for young children to develop naturally according to their age and individual stage of development. By giving young children the scope to choose their own play environment indoors and out, practitioners can build up a picture of where a child is happiest and what really motivates them. This is called free-flow play and can be defined as play when the children choose or decide on how to engage themselves and with what. It is described as open-ended and allows children to have a sense of individualism and an opportunity to make decisions. Then through careful and sensitive intervention at the appropriate moment the practitioner can provide specific support and encouragement to challenge the child to further develop and extend their play. Through staff discussion at planning meetings these threads are refined further into challenging one-to-one, small group and whole group activities and experiences. This provides a sort of pedagogical mortar between the learning building blocks, which children choose for themselves.

The child- and adult-initiated activities and experiences intermesh as an ongoing tapestry leading to further free-flow and adult-led activities. The other unpredictable factor in this process is the weather outdoors which can act as a catalyst for play and learning even without any extra resources being added. The pattern of the year, the seasons and time embroider into this tapestry. Children use their own observations and experiences from life in their play so a child who has come from a country with very different weather or a child who remembers the last time it snowed will demonstrate unique responses. Practitioners can reflect upon these significant experiences and each child's self-chosen free-flow play. One child may be very wary of going outside whilst another may not want to come indoors. As Tina Bruce points out in her 'Twelve Features of Play' in *Time to Play in Early Childhood Education* (1991), a child cannot be made to play and their agenda may or may not be shared. Equally they may be deeply involved and find it hard to leave their deep learning if the practitioners try to draw them into story or mealtime.

The role of the practitioner is to ensure the freedom and individuality of free-flow play that enables each child to progress at his/her own developmental pace. It gives children practice in choosing, developing mastery and in dealing with the consequences of choice and it encourages a more flexible and open-ended use of the school/setting's resources. However, like all genuine freedom, it takes a lot of effort on the part of practitioners. The practitioner role with free-flow play is complex and varied as Dunkin and Hanna's (2001) *Thinking Together* research demonstrates. These include the facilitator who sustains and extends play through scaffolding with new ideas or strategies; the co-learner/explorer who models possible roles a child can take; the play partner who follows the child's lead; the listener/decoder who by giving the child their full attention often acts as a sounding board for ideas and actions as well as paraphrasing language. Finally, the planner role who builds up a child's interests or strengths through guided interaction.

Practitioners and children can both initiate play. Adult-led activities are not 'play' but they can instigate further play and develop it. The role of the practitioner is to help the children develop high functioning free-flow play. This can be achieved by:

- Organising the play environments indoors and out so they are indirectly structuring environments indoors and out through careful attention to the organisation of resources so they are accessible to the children.
- Indirectly structuring the use of time using carefully chosen moments for adult-led activities.
- Participating in the children's self-chosen play wherever appropriate. This is necessary as play can involve morals, ethics, values and power and there are times when children need support in developing positive relationships, attitudes and just actions.

The importance of growing independence

It is important that children are equipped for life and encouraged to be independent from their early years. Practitioners have a crucial role to play in supporting the independence skills of each child. If you do everything for the child they do not learn as they think that you do it better so there is no point in trying. Children can enter nursery standing scarecrow-like waiting for their coats to be removed or put on by well meaning parents and carers until practitioners gently point out that they must try to do it for themselves as this is how they learn. This 'learned helplessness' can be the normal expectation across whole settings/schools if practitioners do everything for children rather than being close by and encouraging, supporting and teaching through appropriate intervention. Dweck's work on 'mastery' and Wood's (1988) theory about children as 'novices' playing around with ideas and 'having a go' at the 'expert' adult roles fits neatly with how children are encouraged to learn and often they end up teaching their parents about their growing skills and independence. Seeing children wearing white laboratory coats (which they put on independently) when being scientists certainly

The role of the adult

shows they take such roles seriously, staring down a microscope, using a magnifying glass or magnet in their own experiments.

Children who are independent take greater responsibility for their own learning and behaviour as well as developing secure self-esteem. They take pride in their skills and are better able to contribute to their groups, school, family and community. Such creative and critical thinking skills plus active learning are highlighted in the revised Early Years Foundation curriculum. This independence alongside effective teaching and learning promotes life-long learning. To enable children's thinking skills practitioners need to consider the provision of:

- Resources, which are easily accessible in suitable storage and clearly labelled and recognised via digital photographs.
- Consistent expectations for children agreed through an Outdoor Play Policy and a few positive rules which young children can learn and carry out in their behaviour, relationships and play.
- Asking open-ended questions such as 'What will we need to help us learn about...', 'Where could we...?' or best of all 'I wonder...?'
- Encouragement for children to self-help and support each other by doing tasks and acting as role models themselves.
- Tasks and specific activities, which are appropriate for individual children and their developmental level, e.g. 'Can you make a den for the Gruffalo?' 'Can you keep teddy dry in the rain?'
- Giving children real responsibility through carrying messages, caring for pets and plants and so on.
- Giving children space to practice their developing skills and abilities ensuring that one activity does not impinge on another, e.g. bicycles are not used in areas where fingers or bare toes might get damaged, or water near books.
- Not automatically solving problems for them but letting them persevere and struggle, co-operate and collaborate before asking for adult involvement. Using phrases such as 'Have you asked any children who are good at joining things together?' or 'Perhaps you need to look indoors in the graphics area...'
- Supporting parents to nurture this child empowerment in a non-threatening way at home rather than doing things for their child because it is easier and quicker, e.g. self-help skills.

Intervening and extending learning

Although free-flow play is a natural process for learning led by the child, it is the interaction by practitioners which can advance young children's thinking and learning both individually and in small groups. Practitioners nurture the development of thinking skills in our children if they:

- Give children time and space to experiment with knowledge and skills they already acquired during free-flow play, e.g. being given play dough ingredients to mix up for themselves rather than having it ready made.

- Help the children to discover things for themselves and see that mistakes are a natural part of the process of their learning and not to be feared.
- Support them in recognising and incorporating new knowledge and skills at the appropriate time and place for each individual, e.g. being taught how to land and roll when jumping from different heights.
- Support them positively in dealing with misfortunes such as falling over and getting wet and how to recover from such negative experiences.
- Work with them to test theories, make propositions and hypotheses as they try out new ideas, e.g. colour paint mixing using the primary colours to make others.
- Provide resources needed to support independent learning, e.g. junk modelling to create role-play props.
- Ensure that children have models of thinkers and independent learners from more experienced peers, visitors and special experiences, e.g. a musician playing an instrument.
- Use the vocabulary of thinking and learning, e.g. using your eyes, ears, voice, brain to....
- Listen carefully and patiently to children's thoughts as they struggle for meaning and sense and not putting words into their mouths.
- Ask open-ended questions and accept innovative answers with sensitivity.
- Model through demonstration the correct and safe use of tools such as woodwork saws and the vice to hold wood. Or asking for another child or adult's help to carry a large, heavy rug for example.
- Give praise and value to children's efforts, suggestions, trials, false starts and successes through phrases such as 'I like the way you helped John move the....'
- Guide them through the process of thinking about thinking, helping them to extend their ability to concentrate and persevere, even when things go wrong, e.g. showing how a specific resource such as a dictionary can be used when unsure of a word.
- Model resilience, thoughtfulness and willingness to listen to the ideas and opinions of others, to make mistakes and learn from them, to be a creative adult who enjoys learning something new.

These ideas have been adapted from Clarke (2007).

Sustained shared thinking, questioning and problem solving outdoors

Researchers use the phrase 'sustained shared thinking' to describe the kind of interactions that best support and extend young children's learning. The formal definition of sustained, shared thinking is 'when two or more individuals work together in an intellectual way to solve a problem, clarify a concept [or] evaluate an activity ... Both parties must contribute to the thinking and it must develop and extend the understanding' (Sylva et al. 2004: 6).

The key findings from the EPPE Report (Effective Provision of Pre-School Education 1997–2003) which looked at the education of over 3,000 children aged between 3 and 4 years old, and spoke to their parents and pre-school settings were that:

The role of the adult

- Settings that have staff who provide children with effective instructive learning environments and use sustained shared thinking to extend children's learning do most to support their learning.
- Children whose thinking skills have been nurtured by supportive practitioners will do better than children whose thinking has been developed alone.

The EPPE report informed the development of questioning and thinking skills by stressing the importance of the following:

- Practitioner 'modelling' is often combined with sustained shared thinking when the practitioner uses verbal commentary, supporting the demonstration of an activity with an interested child by 'thinking out loud', making things explicit and helping to extend the children's vocabulary making the child aware of what they have been learning, e.g. 'If I put this on top of that block will it balance, or should I.....'
- Open-ended questioning is also associated with better outcomes for children's learning through the practitioner and child sharing ideas together, pondering about what's going on, exchanging thoughts and working out problems together, thus deepening the child's understanding of the world.
- The balance of child- and adult-led activities was about equal in who initiated the activities especially when practitioner join in children's play, using humour and being playful thus demonstrating respect whilst deepening the bonds between adults and children.
- The way practitioners intervene and extend child-initiated activities was crucial via making suggestions to develop the scope and direction of an activity. By asking questions a practitioner can help the child to develop and extend an activity, helping them to make links with other areas of learning and encouraging them to create their own challenges. This is called scaffolding.

These techniques help to develop the child's confidence in being a learner and encourage the child to be involved in his or her own learning. For example, in deconstruction a child spent the whole morning totally absorbed in taking apart an amplifier leading to the child asking questions for the practitioner to answer such as 'How can I get inside this box?', 'I can't undo it, can you come and start me off?' and 'What do these do?'

By gradually transferring responsibility to succeed, the practitioner enables the child develop their own independence. Such an approach can also be supported by the workshop area approach indoors and out so children can help themselves to materials and take charge of their own learning. Once they have learnt and practised the skills, they can tackle more challenging activities independently including relationship issues such as dealing with frustration and anger, as well as learning to talk through conflicts and dealing with others' anger.

To provide quality interaction

A vibrant outdoor learning environment is important for children to develop their communication, language, thinking, social and emotional skills alongside developing independence of self-help skills. The zones indoors and outside provide for rich investigation, exploration and interaction with others both child and adult. Practitioners deal sensitively with children's play and relationships in particular when they are having difficulty coping with their own feelings and frustrations when coming to terms with similarities and differences and in forming friendships as Feinberg and Minders (1994) highlighted. Practitioners can converse with children throughout the day in a wide range of ways but children are much more likely to initiate and respond when they trust the adult and understand that the adult is really interested in them and what they have to say. They are also more likely to engage if they know that the practitioner will not take over their play and redirect for their purposes. The practitioner can support talk and interaction between children by playing alongside them and giving commentary to the actions and experiences. Lucas and Claxton (2010: 115) very clearly describe the importance of children's thinking being nurtured and enhanced by this social learning and what they describe as collective intelligence so they come to understand more about how the world works within a community of learners. The richest conversations often take place in dens, tipis and hidey-holes such as 'caves'. These are 'wild' places where children can hide with a friend or two and be between worlds as they feel they are unseen and out of the adult scaffolding. The interaction between the children as they talk about things from their agendas provides the practitioner with further knowledge of how to extend them through stories and traditional tales enacted through socio-dramatic play in different scales. Research also supports that children whose first language is not English are also more likely to talk outside rather than in. Using small role-play figures in a sink garden planted with slow growing conifers and small rocks can cover many of the prime and specific areas of the EYFS curriculum as well as supporting particular learning characteristics and social/emotional development.

An example of quality interaction

Following a visit from a real mountaineer who brought all his special clothing, equipment and showed a film of his climbing adventures, two girls are exploring small role-play in the sink garden. Rabia and Hattie are playing in the sink garden using several small figures. They have sustained their involvement in a game of their own creation and are happy playing together despite one child being far less confident in speaking English.

Hattie says: 'There are two climbers at the top of the mountain and another waiting here down in their camp at the bottom.' She places them on the tallest rock demonstrating appropriate positional language as well as numerical understanding and some concepts of size. She continues: 'They walked a long way through the dark Christmas tree forest and this man is tired.' Pointing to the one at the bottom. She is also able to move and manipulate the figures carefully and communicates her knowledge of mountains and forests.

Rabia meanwhile has sustained her involvement more quietly but with avid interest. The practitioner has observed them for several minutes and has noticed that Rabia has placed another figure under a smaller stone saying quietly 'His house.' The practitioner says, 'I wonder if all these mountain explorers are together. Perhaps one is lost? How will he find his friends?' Rabia smiles at this intervention and rushes indoors to the graphics area. She returns after several minutes with a piece of paper saying delightedly 'He not lost, he in the tent!' pointing at the smaller rock. The practitioner smiles and responds 'Well done! How will he find his friends?' Rabia gives her the piece of paper on which are several clear shapes corresponding to the rocks and stones and a series of dots between them. 'My map help him!' Rabia announces. The practitioner is curious to know how Rabia has understood one of the purposes of maps and asks her how she knows about maps. Rabia replies 'My Daddy.' Hattie had listened to the conversation and asks 'Rabia can my explorers use your map to get down the mountain safely?' Rabia nods her agreement and together they march the remaining mountaineers down to the base of the mountain.

Knowing when to intervene

A practitioner collaborating and intervening with the child can lead to a huge range of possible experiences. However, the challenge *is when* to intervene to extend the quality of play and learning. All children need time to explore and extend their play and learning for themselves as well as opportunities to revisit and practice several times over. Each time a child repeats something they generally use different resources or play with different peers or adapt ideas thus building upon their previous experience. They also arrange resources in different and often increasingly complex ways. They talk and collaborate about their play with greater engagement and attention to detail too. Sometimes there will be conflicts, which may be about sharing resources or inappropriate behaviours. In learning how to assert themselves appropriately by giving reasons and using phrases such as 'Stop it! I don't like it because...' children start to manage very well by themselves with a sensitive adult nearby. This then gives them some control over their play, who is involved and when it ends. How often do some children want to play with the Halloween/Mexican Day of the Dead resources at Christmas time or do others start wrapping presents up until Saint Valentine's Day? Child development and learning is unique to each individual and thus needs a similarly individual approach by practitioners too.

Intervention is a subtle and intuitive skill, which requires high quality observation and thoughtful language. The 'teachable moment' can be fleeting but is vital in the effective intervention and establishment of high quality. Thus in order to explore possibilities, practitioners can use a variety of means: giving commentary to children's play and learning; encouraging children to describe, explain, and sequence their ideas; creating scenarios, questions and provocations for them to explore, explain, hypothesise about; talk about problems and encourage reflections; let them help in making decisions and in practical tasks such as tidying up as well as involving them in planning changes particularly to the outdoors as their ideas may be life changing.

Whilst practitioners do need to be involved with children's play to support it, the children themselves often display that refreshing honesty of telling you when to go away. Therefore practitioners need to listen carefully and reflect as to why they are joining in and how in terms of time, space and resources their intervention will add quality to the learning.

Working in close partnership with parents, family members and other professionals about risk and challenge

Practitioners work with families by building up close relationships. This starts at the very first meeting and particularly during the induction period when a child is starting into a setting or school. In this period the parents/carers are sharing their knowledge of their child and their interests, needs, likes and dislikes as well as broader information about the family structure, medical information and contact details. When families first visit your school or setting you should consider sharing your values and ethos with them so that they start to understand the value and importance of playing and learning outside. Whilst there will not be time for in-depth understanding it is important that parents feel comfortable with what is on offer most of the time and that it is akin to what they as good and caring parents want for their child. Risk, challenge and adventure are sadly not for everyone. In some settings/schools this starts as a home visit to see the child in their familiar environment whilst in others it may be in a previous setting. It is an ongoing process and ideally a two-way process of information sharing. Its success hinges upon the professional sensitivity of the practitioner to respect the parents and follow their lead as far as is reasonable. In the early days the parent/carer is still likely to be on site and able to add and expand the practitioner's knowledge of their child by providing more background as to why and how their child plays and learns. This means that if a practitioner learns that a child loves playing with dolls they will try to ensure that dolls are available in the home corner inside and possibly in prams and buggies outdoors so the child has something familiar to play with from the start. This then could be extended through small role-play figures in the dolls house or garage to widen the play to another scale and with other children to develop sharing.

Ultimately the practitioner must try their utmost to work with the parents in order to have a positive impact on the child's development and learning. Underpinning this are the cornerstones of good two-way communication within a welcoming atmosphere, respect for the diversity and individuality of families and a culture of learning together about the child and their progress so it can be further enabled through shared contributions. This firm foundation of trusting relationships should then continue into the transition to the child's next steps into the reception class and beyond.

Certain children and families will need far greater sensitivity and professional engagement due to special needs, different languages and in some cases child protection issues. In these situations other external practitioners and professionals will also be involved and their views, knowledge and reports will need careful consideration. Building relationships with these more complex families will often take longer but once established are very important in underpinning the child's development and progress. Small steps are usually the way forward for the practitioner in gaining the parents confidence and demonstrating new ideas for joint working to enable the child to benefit. Children with individual special needs may need greater time to settle and the practitioner will liaise closely on a daily basis with the child's family either face to face or perhaps via a home-setting book system to make sense of what a child is doing. Children and families from different language backgrounds may need the support of a translator or advice from external experts in the case of refugees and asylum seekers.

The role of the adult

Although child development is a well-documented sequence it may become evident that a particular child has unique needs that have not been diagnosed. This may then require the utmost professionalism on the part of the practitioner and possibly the need to get parents to agree to external professional support from an educational psychologist, social worker etc.

Occasionally parents may be reticent to provide information due to complex issues such as imprisonment, abuse, divorce, separation or bereavement. Such situations will require the practitioner to be very delicate whilst trying to ascertain the needs of the child in order to ensure their safety and also providing the most appropriate care and education.

Promoting inclusion through equality of opportunity and anti-discriminatory practice

The outdoors provides a rich basis to childhood with the opportunity to experience things on a different scale and in different ways to indoor provision. Children can play with different children in different ways and have fun getting wet, dirty and in different dimensions, which are simply not feasible indoors. They experience awe and wonder with the changing seasons, weather and wildlife. They develop a vast array of life skills, which will lead to future life opportunities. This is a moral right for all children.

Practitioners need to carefully consider equality, diversity and challenge to ensure an inclusive yet diverse range of culturally and gender wide resources are available indoors and out and that the images portrayed are sensitive. Children learn so much from just observing. If we only provide them with English home corner resources children from other backgrounds may interpret their own home as being of less or different value. Refugee children in particular may need to see familiar home items to help them deal with stress and trauma. Setting up a tent or a caravan outside, for example, can be so enlightening for all as well as a means of valuing the home background of traveller families. Such play can of course create new learning at the same time for other children less familiar with the resources.

Gender and adventure, risk and challenge

Whilst gender is explored fully in Chapter 4, the importance of equality has been shown to impact particularly on the behaviour of boys' play when staff are not involved. Davies (1991) found that boys took longer to adjust to nursery and form attachments than girls. As practitioners were not spending as much time playing in the areas where the boys tended to play, they had fewer opportunities to develop positive attitudes and learn with them. Gender research is an area of fierce debate and stereotyping but research has shown that boys in particular are at risk of becoming disaffected as they often choose to spend longer periods of time out-of-doors engaged in high levels of physical activity. However, as Helen Bilton points out non-stereotypical play should include all children and provide models promoting positive challenges for all whether over protected or not.

The differing needs of boys and girls

We know that from birth, gender differences become apparent certainly from different socialisation experiences, which are difficult to tease out. For example, we are told that new born boys weigh more than girls and are slightly longer. They are also reported to cry more and tend to be more demanding. Baby girls are generally stronger and more responsive to the human voice, which is why it is thought they talk sooner. As their brains and central nervous systems develop sooner, girls often control their bladders and bowels at a much earlier age. Girls tend to be more sociable than boys, but they are also more emotional in their relationships. Boys are inclined to be more boisterous, outgoing and competitive, but more prone to language and behaviour problems. This is because the cerebral cortex, which is crucial in the development of memory, attention, language and motor co-ordination, develops sooner in girls. Hence they tend to read and write sooner, use language more effectively and perform better academically than boys in school. These differences generally level out by puberty. Boys are generally better at using the right sides of their brains and are therefore usually better at spatial tasks such as puzzles, and ball games as well as being less fearful in exploration but no doubt this too is affected by socialisation. We therefore need to plan activities indoors and out which have relevance to both boys and girls, build their confidence and self-esteem and motivate them.

In the nursery age group evidence has shown that girls tend to be drawn to activities which involve adults, whilst boys tend to be drawn to activities such as construction, climbing and gross-motor skills. As a female-dominated profession we have to be very aware of our own socialisation and how we 'see' girls and boys. We need to carefully reflect on how we organise play activities to provide for all children as we are all unique with different societal norms and expectations. Our personal preferences from our own socialisation must not distract us from providing for the interests and needs of both boys and girls in order to maximise their true potential.

Individual and unique needs

There are some individual children who have very unique learning needs. Some children will have a legal entitlement because of their disabilities, medical or special needs to extra adult support or specific resources. These children will have special planning documents which practitioners discuss, develop and share with the child's parents and other professionals to ensure they access a rich and balanced early years curriculum by individual pathways. It is through carefully considered challenges and stimulating experiences that children with individual needs really prosper. Their progression in the areas of learning can particularly benefit outdoors in terms of locomotor development, e.g. walking, running, jumping, climbing and non-locomotor such as bending, stretching, rolling, stopping, balancing. Their manipulative skills and co-ordination also benefit from a huge range of permutations. For example, throwing: one can throw high and low; hard and soft; throw while standing or running; throw forwards, sideways and backwards; throw and bounce etc. Planning for these experiences can emerge from both free-flow play and specific adult-led activities to nurture these and other skills for particular individuals.

The role of the adult

Other children will demonstrate particular abilities, skills and talents in certain aspects of learning. Such able, gifted and talented children may also need individualised planning and support so they do not become bored and frustrated. If a child is very comfortable in particular areas of expertise they may not be keen to expand on these and need specific support to access the full range of possible learning opportunities outside.

Practitioners must consider the child first and their need or disability second. By observing their current abilities and interests you are in a far better position to offer the most supportive relationships, intervention and scaffolding as well as the best balance of free-flow and adult-led activities.

Summary

The role of the practitioner and their professional skills in relationships, pedagogy and practice reinforce and strengthen the progress of each child as well as the positive belief each parent has in their child. The sound use of observation, assessment, planning and evaluation strengthens the many ways a child engages with people and their environment. Once positive relationships and broad experiences to nurture the characteristics of learning are established, the fundamental prime areas of learning flourish and lead into the development of the numerous skills, knowledge and understanding of the specific areas.

Environment

Introduction

The environment for young children in an early years setting includes both indoors and out. It also involves the local environment as a third classroom outside as this can be a 'teacher' in its own right and provide experiences which then free up practitioners to observe children in depth and spend quality time with them teaching and learning. Both indoors and outdoors should provide a varied range of open-ended opportunities which enrich and enliven children's lives as they interact, play and learn.

This chapter looks at what the environment is, why it is special and how it can assist us in facilitating and extending children's experiences of risk, challenge and adventure. It discusses both the indoor and outdoor environments and the types of opportunities and provision that should ideally be available to help support and extend children's learning effectively. Finally it considers the relationship between the indoor and outdoor environments and how these can work together to ensure free-flow play.

What constitutes the environment?

The environment consists of the resources, people and local surroundings which provide opportunities for interaction and learning for a young child. This will include the premises (indoors and out) where the child is, the local area outside and people in the community. The Early Years Foundation Stage (2012) places great emphasis upon the environment describing it as a theme – 'Enabling Environments'. The term 'enabling' allows for openness and flexibility which is essential when considering how to link a child's interests with what is available indoors, outdoors and locally.

The document *Development Matters in the Early Years Foundation Stage* (Department for Education 2012: 3) states that an 'Enabling Environment' should value all people and learning. Enabling environments are broadly the range of resources, people and experiences that a child interacts with. Within these enabling environments children learn and develop well in ways supported and extended by partnership between practitioners and parents or carers. 'Enabling Environments' should offer:

- stimulating resources, relevant to all the children's cultures and communities;

- rich learning opportunities through play and playful teaching; and
- support for children to take risks and explore.

Practitioners working in the early years therefore should plan and provide both indoor and outdoor environments which connect with and are focused on high quality play, learning and teaching. As Helen Bilton (2002: 1) concisely explains: 'The environment is, therefore, the means by which knowledge and the child are linked; it forms part of the education equation and as such has to be planned carefully.'

Enabling environments both indoors and out should work in symbiosis to ensure that not only the children's interests and needs are underpinned, supported and extended but also that they act in a linked fashion via free-flow play to provide and extend every opportunity for adventure, risk and challenge. The physical environments should offer:

- space in as many dimensions as is safe and feasible;
- accessibility;
- stability and consistency of rules and expectations;
- high quality resources and adult teaching; and
- play and learning potential through a variety of provocations including adult- and child-initiated activities, displays and interactions.

These should also be designed to promote learning across all the areas of the EYFS.

The emotional environment is also crucial because until children feel safe, loved and have positive self-esteem they will not feel comfortable about taking risks and rising to new challenges. The emotional environment must be considered wherever a child is and should offer:

- warmth and love;
- positive mental health;
- wellbeing;
- recognition of the uniqueness of each child's individuality, competence, capability, resilience and self-assurance;
- fun!

This will result in happy, confident children who learn easily and naturally as they are comfortable within their environment and with the people who care for them.

The indoor environment

Places speak to us. Long corridors whisper 'run' to a young child whilst fences invite them to run a stick along to make a sound. The furniture and physical resources give unseen messages of warmth, pleasure, fear, stay away etc. Spaces and colours also speak to the emotions. Therefore the indoor environment is much more than the physical setting. It includes all the external factors and conditions which potentially can influence a child. This includes the people within it, how time is structured, how behaviour is encouraged or discouraged and how roles and responsibilities are distributed. We do not usually take into account how different we are, for example, at home to at work, let alone on the bus in-between. Think how confusing this change of environments must be for young children. The difference in a child's behaviour between home and setting often confuses parents and practitioners but it is often due to the different environments. The indoor environment is a launch pad for each child moving from their home to the setting as it will include resources which are easily recognised and familiar. It offers good learning experiences which encompass a range of developmental levels, learning styles and individual interests. This is not only through the rich array of resources but also how they can be used, e.g. quietly, actively, solo or socially to provide novelty and challenge in a simple or increasing complex manner depending upon the individual child.

The indoor environment usually consists of different spaces within which young children learn from their actions and interactions. An environment rich in experience should beckon the child to play and invite him or her to be curious, discover more and make meaning. Good indoor spaces for children must supply experience of comfort and security, freedom and direction, mobility and autonomy, trial and error, safety, health and risk, privacy and social space alongside order and some structure in the form of rituals and routines. Children also need people, as it is through people that children learn to become members of society.

Adults have three important roles in terms of the environment:

- Environmental planner
- Environmental participant
- Environmental evaluator.

A well-planned, supportive environment liberates adults to care and teach, to observe and ask questions at the right time, to provide the smile or nod or cuddle at the best moment. Staff walk a tightrope of setting up the environment, sometimes proposing specific activities whilst observing how the child reacts before deciding what to focus on to extend the child's thinking. It is the skill of the adult in understanding what is going on in the child's head at each moment which determines what the environment develops into next. The adult needs to talk with the child to gain their ideas and perspectives. According to Susan Isaacs, 'A child has little power for sustaining conversation as such, and needs other opportunity to talk with people who talk well. Grown ups or older children who will listen to what he has to say and respond appropriately are of far more value to him than specific lessons in clear speech' (Weber 1971: 179).

We each have a vision for children and what we want them to be. It is certain that they will need to become resourceful, loving human beings with a positive sense of self-esteem to win and lose, create, produce and learn independently. If we provide them with prison-like environments barricaded against the world, the outcomes will be different from if they are provided with light airy spaces with easy access to the outdoors full of awe, wonder and possible adventures.

Environmental aspects to consider indoors

Space, scale, size and time

All spaces have size, scale, aesthetic qualities, entries and pathways which work together to give the environment its feel. Scale is important in that if children feel lost they find

Environment

places to be more secure whereas those who get used to openness are characterised by their desire to move around.

Size is less importance than our perception of it, however, it must be fit for purpose as Montessori pioneered in her 'child scaling' of furniture. This should also be applied to sinks and other fixtures for ease of access etc. If you sit on the floor or a child's chair within an indoor environment you gain a perspective of their environment as seen through their eyes. It is not only the physical space which is important, but the smell, sound, temperature and humidity. A hot, crowded room will be noisy, smelly and far less bearable than the same sized room with fewer people in it. Having the choice to move inside and out gives each child the opportunity to choose what best suits them.

Time is another factor. If you remember your own school days, feelings of oppression and imprisonment are often recalled whereas the long days of summer holidays appear to grow in length.

Aesthetic considerations

A pleasant multi-sensory environment that is visual, aural or tactile can be achieved through displays and how the furniture and resources are arranged in relation to light, access and proximity to other different areas. This is particularly important for the children who may not experience much beauty and good design in their lives. The feel of wood or fabric, the line and design of furniture as well as a rich array of objects and pictures with aesthetic qualities rather than a jumble of ill-sorted objects makes a significant difference. Storage and furniture has a key role too especially if made of high quality, long lasting materials such as the Community Playthings range.

Sound

Sound can soothe or jar both adults and children in terms of talking and laughing as well as music. Ideally there should be areas which allow for calm and quiet as well as areas where noise making is the expectation.

Colour and light

Colour can reflect moods and highlight features with some having calming effects such as blue. Bright walls can draw children to spaces and white makes spaces feel larger. It is important to think about the use of primary colours on walls and flooring as colour is far more easily added to a light coloured or plain background by incorporating fabric, paintings or photographs. Whatever colours are used they should not assault the senses and overload everyone. Natural light should be used whenever possible and it is generally best to avoid harsh fluorescent lighting. Lighting can give space warmth and character as well as highlighting certain areas. The use of large 'institutional' wall murals and 'cute' commercial art images can act as unfortunate barriers and create inflexible areas as well as giving unintended negative perceptions of children. More often than not a 'homelike' inviting environment leads to children giving objects and equipment the fullest appreciation along with the care and respect they deserve.

Character and architecture

Character comes from the architecture, furnishings and woodwork plus the resources and how they are arranged. These should encourage children's involvement in a space or zone for an activity. The zones or areas which broadly cover a rich and balanced curriculum usually include:

- sand (ideally both wet and dry);
- water play;
- tactile and manipulative activities;
- language and book corner;
- graphics and mark making;
- music and sound;
- dance and movement;
- construction;
- creative and making area;
- home corner and dramatic play area;
- small role-play;
- maths/science discovery area;
- ICT.

These areas or zones are important as they ensure curriculum coverage alongside a broad and balanced range of starting points for children's own interests and needs.

Therefore good space offers character and flexibility. Always provide small spaces within larger ones and consider the possibilities of multi-level space to provide greater flexibility without sacrificing familiar features which help children and adults feel 'at home' and yet able to explore and discover more.

Flow

Flow is a key concept in this nurturing and challenging process as it can capitalise on a child's engagement, fascination, desire or interest and take it much further. The pathways, relationships and movement between activity areas should support children's need for a range of experiences indoors and out such as self-chosen quiet time, a sense of order and calm, a feeling of belonging, participation in collaborative activity, achievement of a particular skill or ability and the chance to make a mess. Quiet areas need to be located together whilst art and craft areas and tactile, water and sand activities need to be near a sink and on a washable floor. This can be challenging for adults as resources can get transported from area to area and moved around between zones. A child who is fascinated by movement through things might start off outside by going through tunnels or a series of large cardboard boxes at different speeds. The child might then move onto racing small balls or cars down plastic tubing or guttering. He or she might then move inside and be drawn (with adult encouragement) to construct a marble run or use weaving or sewing materials to thread beads. Young children are born creative and inventive and enabling them to move easily between areas to continue their exploration and discovery allows for wonderful learning experiences and the satisfaction and sense of flow from learning autonomously.

Environment
Existing structures

Structural aspects should be taken advantage of such as an interesting view or nooks and crannies which can be used as dens and retreat spaces. How each area is developed will then in turn affect the choice of nearby activity spaces. High use areas should be spread throughout the total available space so that the children will be more inclined to play in small groups or as individuals rather than creating 'bottle neck' activities where little of value is achieved due to pressure of numbers.

Pathways

Pathways are very important in terms of making spaces work. Pathways are 'the empty spaces on the floor or ground through which people move from one place to another' (Kritchevsky et al. 1977). Once activity areas are planned it is important to consider the movement between these from the children's point of view. It helps children decide on their focus and set their own goals if they know where they can find things. This also means they can then transfer items between areas if needed and return them later. In order to self-regulate they need to know where the quiet, reflective spaces are as well as the busy, noisy ones and the spaces where they can have a cuddle with an adult or a quiet nap. Clear paths and adequate empty space are crucial to good organisation and learning. Adults can identify these areas by crouching down low, sitting and exploring at the child's height to ensure no apparatus blocks pathways. (Outdoors this can be sometimes achieved by different textures.)

Boundaries and enclosures

These can be created around activity areas to create a sense of order and help children make real choices in their play and become more deeply involved for longer periods of time. An array of brightly coloured furniture can help keep equipment in certain areas but from the child's viewpoint it can be a visual distraction. The use of transparent fabrics or shelving as partial dividers can give children a sense of privacy whilst still allowing a degree of supervision. Large cushions, boxes and containers covered in blankets and rugs can also offer excellent boundaries. For babies, lined large dog baskets are ideal as baby sleeping nests and play areas, which can be crawled in and out of.

Chairs and tables

Very few young children need to actually sit but if we want them to experiment and explore different media, construct, create and play games we need to provide appropriate surfaces at different heights. Furniture is essential for meals and more complex manipulative tasks, but most activities can be enjoyed lower down on the floor, on PVC cloths, blocks, boxes or low tables. Carpet covered risers are excellent for babies and children learning to walk. Changes in height can also make available spaces seem larger. Any low space such as a den should also be considered for adequate adult access as should suitable seating as children tend to gather where adults are.

Storage

Crook and Farmer (1996) state that the presentation of equipment and resources should say '"come and get me", inspiring feelings of excitement, intrigue and the desire to explore.' The creativity of the staff team along with careful use of soft furnishings, photographs, labels, baskets, containers, display and shelving can remove visual clutter and support children's engagement and focus everywhere. It can often assist them in tidying up too! Less is often more as when the amount of resources available are pared back it allows adults to keep areas inviting and exciting so that they will be utilised far more effectively by children. Effective storage maximises the use of resources and helps children to understand the benefits of order.

Storage can be categorised as open or closed or visible and accessible. The former is generally out-of-sight or reach to unauthorised users and includes special equipment, one-off resources or precious items which need adult supervision. Visible and accessible storage is available to all potential users. Storage can be fixed or movable. Containers on casters allow flexibility within an environment as well as special access at different times and places. Multi-use or specialised storage allows for special items such as large blocks or books to be transported and moved safely. Ideally storage should be next to the area or zone it relates to and be able to comfortably hold and display its contents. In order to be effective it needs to be the correct size and shape for the space and the users as well as aesthetically pleasing.

Mixed-aged settings

These provide particular challenges for adults as children who are at least a year apart in a family grouping will have considerably different needs and interests which can lead to potential conflicts and lost opportunities. There is also a danger of providing only for the lowest common denominator or restricting the physical development of the younger babies and children. There should therefore be some spaces specifically for babies, toddlers and older children alongside larger shared spaces. Low boundaries can create spaces which 'house' the very youngest with their need for close adult involvement but give them the chance to observe their older peers. In such settings tables with rims or storage bins in the centre can provide good surfaces for older children's learning. Loft areas can offer very young children exciting space underneath in an interesting enclosure whilst providing access to the upper area for older and physically competent children.

Display

Displays should be used to arouse curiosity. This can be achieved by including different styles, cultures and mediums of materials and images. One or two children's paintings are often more meaningful than a mass of images and highlight learning better. Noticeboards need to be uncluttered and attractive and have regular updates to maintain adult interest. Displays using laminated images or box frames can also be used very effectively outside.

Environment

Entrance areas

Well-designed entries and exits allow for calm physical and emotional movement even in emergencies. Foyers and open spaces need to be welcoming and comfortable to both children and adults. Windows, displays and personal welcomes are crucial. Factors such as safe storage of buggies and outdoor clothing should also be planned for.

Why the outdoor environment matters

It is the elements of free-flow play, the freedom of choice to engage in particular interests or fascinations and to a certain extent the lack of predictability outdoors, which makes it so essential for young children. Outdoors is not easily sanitised but it is a firm foundation for real experience and that includes grazed knees! Increasingly life is planned and organised for children often with little regard to their individual development. Researchers such as Jerome Kagan (1994), Frank F. Furstenberg (1988) and David Elkind (1987) all have pointed to the hyper concerns of parents leading to increased anxiety, delayed adulthood and the inability to engage with new ideas and cope with stress in young people. Some discomfort and disappointment are as critical in the development of all young children as much as joy, awe and wonder and are far more likely to be experienced outside rather than in.

Outdoors provides many rich and exciting opportunities for active motor play and to discover and investigate through a range of natural materials and resources not easily available at home. Children need time and freedom to explore outdoors with the practitioners observing them but also trusting them to follow their own instincts and interests. This important element of freedom particularly in make-believe play was richly described as long ago as 1938, by Ella Ruth Boyce (1938: 185) working in Stepney, London. Boyce describes how giving the children increasing freedom to play with minimal adult interference led after initial behaviour difficulties to more imaginative play and richer personalities. The reduction of human interference and relative disorder outside is attractive to children as it allows them to move freely and make more mess than would be practical or permissible indoors.

Natural environments are highly dynamic and give children the chance to learn more about their bodies and to change things discovered through digging, building, climbing, splashing, breaking and balancing. This gives them far greater control and involvement in their own play and learning. Children can interact with their environment and learn things they could never achieve indoors. They use natural materials such as earth, wood sticks, sand, stones and leaves to follow their imaginations in a larger, free space. They think more openly and are less restricted by adult rules about mess, noise and space. Richard Louv (2005: 3, 7) supports this approach in his comment 'Just as children need good nutrition and adequate sleep, they may very well need contact with nature.' Children gain immediate information about the world around them through playful interaction with nature such as how their bodies work, how they collaborate or not with others and then test these ideas again and again helping to build their self-confidence and intellectual skills.

The outdoors provides the experiences which are essential in the creation of self-regulating children. It can calm the very active and provide genuine physical struggle for those who need to enhance their gross and fine-motor skills. Others will gain mastery of skills, extend their motivation, learn to model and support others whilst developing an understanding of what they are capable. It also helps teach life skills such as hazard awareness and when to ask for help.

Why is the outside special for young children?

For some children the sheer physical freedom and tactile experience of feeling the sun, wind, snow or rain on their skin not only adds to the achievement of flow but also helps them achieve an early spiritual experience. Particularly for children with special needs and those with complex disabilities there is often far greater physical reaction outside than when cosseted in the warmth of the classroom.

A garden or outdoor play space can also provide young children with something special that they own and respect whilst developing a sense of place. A sense of place builds upon their understanding of their own home and gives them a different range of possible connections to learning opportunities which interest them. A sense of place is important as Derr's 2002 research shows demonstrating the importance of connections in children's lives between themselves and their peers, their families and their community. Derr identifies four broad themes of play related to children's sense of place:

- Four wheelers, ramps and rites of passage – children who learn through adventure, risk-taking, experimentation, exploration and self created rites of passage.
- Fort makers – children who experience imagination, escape, safety and creativity through the structure they create.
- Carers – the children who learn nurturance, companionship, respect, awe and wonder from animals, plants, gardening, weather and elements of nature.
- Web builders – children who have reasons to stay or to go, who understand rootedness versus transience. Those who value deep rooted almost spiritual relationships.

Young children's rapid brain development is enhanced by them forming strong connections, and because their experiences are limited to their surroundings, the environment we provide for them has a crucial impact on the manner in which their brains develop.

Research by Titman (1994); Moore and Wong (1997); and Fjortoft (2004) shows that natural or wild environments are more interesting to children because they offer a wide range of options for encounters in diverse topologies with differing textures and child-sized spaces to hide in and explore. For many children space, time and opportunity to experience the elements, different weathers and seasons is very valuable as they can lack such opportunities in their family lives.

What should the environment look like outdoors?

When designing an outdoor environment the children should be involved from the start. At Chelsea Open Air we started by asking the children which features they wanted to keep in the original garden and not surprisingly one was the huge old tree which lay across the garden which had unique play features with limitless possibilities. Many years on that same fallen tree is still being used in a variety of creative, flexible ways daily and it cost nothing!

Any space has possibilities for a young child even with very little in it. Give a small group a giant cardboard box and you will be amazed at what it becomes and how they develop their play. So do not worry if you are not blessed with a large space. What you can do is audit what you have already and then discuss what else might be possible.

If you are designing or redesigning your outside area there are certain elements to consider first such as:

- pathways or routes around;
- access to toilets, clothing and indoors;
- storage;
- what the materials and textures to add for both aesthetic and exploratory play possibilities;
- how active and quieter areas/zones fit together to avoid conflicts;
- physical features such as sand, mud and water;
- areas for gardening;
- active fixed features such as slides, balancing, swinging and climbing;
- movable and wheeled toys;
- open or slack spaces;
- areas for trees and bushes.

You may also need to be creative in how the outside links to the inside with covered areas for books, for example, which will need to remain dry.

Areas of the outdoor environment

Any outdoor space should be open-ended but also provide areas or zones just like the indoors which then easily enable different sorts of play and learning to take place.

These areas or zones should provide the basis of the long-term core provision but will be unique to each setting. The real benefits of having certain fixed provision as well as zones is that in less inclement weather you do not need to add much in terms of resourcing. There needs to be careful consideration of space so that that bare feet do not get run over by bikes, or quiet talk and stories are not disturbed by exuberant rough and tumble games. Children do not see these areas/zones as we do and the invisible boundaries that adults can create between them can be a cause of conflict. Zones could include:

- Sand pit area with water, boat, den/play house and table area.
- Natural and created climbing, balancing, swinging and sliding area.
- Environment/wild area with a willow den, grid covered pond, bird table, log pile, compost maker, insect houses etc.
- Gardening area designed and themed in planting by the children for growing vegetables.

- Gathering area with decking or benches for community times or used for singing, music, stories, puppets and plays.
- A mud kitchen for making mud pies, moulding etc.
- An area which can be flooded with water as a paddling pool.
- A quieter area, which acts as a 'bridge' for small role-play, construction, office, books, creative activities etc.
- Covered area or walkway which can be used for storage whatever the weather but has access to power so woodwork, lap tops, microscopes and floor robots can be used there.
- A larger covered area with accessible storage which can be used for different scales of obstacle courses and physical activities such as dance, parachute, role-play, large block construction, and experiences when the weather is very wet.
- Open space for bikes, skipping, jumping, running, physical activities, balls, bats, hoops and skittles.

I am also keen on the term 'slack space' mentioned by Watts (2011) who describes it as originating in a 'Play England' booklet and is used to describe a space with no predetermined function or purpose. I like this concept as in a sense any area or zone has the adults purpose attached to it whilst in reality the children make of it whatever they want. These areas are very flexible, fluid and open-ended and therefore respond very easily to a diverse range of children from toddlers to seven year olds. Children can gain experience on different scales and through different sizes of group involvement alone or together. We have to look carefully at what is there naturally, what we provide and why in relation to the children's interests and needs as well as an appropriate balance and flow of opportunities.

Finally, Sobell (1990, 1996) talks about 'special places' for children that have the following features:

- They are often found and constructed by children themselves without fear of adult interference.
- They remain essentially secret and known only to those who create them.
- They adapt via their owners decisions and imaginations.
- They are safe for children.
- They empower their builders.
- They are organised worlds.
- The zones are separate and yet connected as they need to link fluidly according to the motivations and interests of the children. Thus if a group create a den they may bring a range of loose parts from the construction zone, the sand or water areas. They may add resources from dramatic play too.

The features of an outdoor environment

An ideal space for risk, challenge and adventure starts with the suggestions from the children, families and practitioners. It should be developmentally appropriate to its users taking into account the separation of active zones from those requiring quieter involvement. Sand areas need access to water and to be separated by hard surfaces to

Environment

avoid slip hazards. Clear boundaries with sufficient space to enter and exit active zones are also important as are suitable circulation pathways throughout. It is useful to bear in mind ease and comfort of use in setting up and clearing away resources and factors such as wind, temperature and landscape features such as fences and trees. The outdoor space should be as open-ended as possible, but also allow for ongoing alteration and semi-destruction through such things as bonfires and annual growth cycles. Ease of maintenance should also be considered so, for example, sand can be raked over easily and replaced when necessary or wood can be preserved and replaced when it starts to rot.

Green structures

A range of small trees and bushes with diverse forms and heights allows for screening, exploratory play and interest in nature. Different varieties of leaf shape and a range of deciduous and non-deciduous plants also helps create year round interest. You can use willow trees to create a tunnel or den, which if watered, will turn green each year.

Loose parts

These include a range of man-made recycled materials such as carpet squares, tyres, boxes, crates, cardboard tubes, reels, guttering and piping, fabric, netting, rope as well as materials to mould, move and use such as earth, sand and water. The UK scrap stores have a range of useful materials exemplified by the Bristol-based Play Pods.

Diverse topography

Winding pathways, slopes, even ground, rough cliffs and flat, smooth surfaces for cycling, running and ball games provide children with different experiences to master in their environment. Slopes can be wonderful for children to roll down. It also gives children real reasons to use positional language in context such as up, down, in-between and next.

Graspable, detached objects

Children should have a range of tools and equipment for throwing, digging, building and playing with. They should be quality resources designed in line with the age and developmental level of the child and could include balls, bats, quoits, kites, spades, buckets, and moulds the list is endless – but do consider accessible storage.

Attached objects

These should be suitable for jumping over, jumping onto and down from as well as balancing on. They can be loose parts such as planks and crate balance beams, tyres, skipping ropes, wood stepping stones or permanent fixed features. Log stumps and cut offs are also very useful and you can add a range of smaller natural objects such as cones, twigs and leaves for symbolic play. If you cannot find these items, a range of companies including Reflections on Learning, Cosy and Early Excellence offer a good choice.

Non-rigid attached objects

These offer places to swing, hang from and climb on such as a rope swing or ladder on a strong branch at an appropriate height and with adequate space surrounding it and surfacing underneath. This should be well tested by a sturdy adult first!

Climbable features

Places to explore and master as well as to climb up on, look out from and descend safely. These can be permanent or moveable features but need to have appropriate height and challenge for the age and developmental needs of the children using them. Big wooden blocks, ladders and beams can be used to link in a variety of exciting ways. Community Playthings have a variety of well made equipment, which is worth exploring.

Shelters or dens

Areas to hide in to experience a secret place for quiet and solitude as well as place to talk and play with peers. These can be permanent structures such as playhouses but fabric sheeting, netting or tarpaulins with clips can also create exciting open-ended and moveable features.

A mud kitchen

This could include mouldable materials, containers and tools for building, shaping or 'cooking.' Recycled kitchen equipment can be really useful here.

Water

Places for children to paddle, splash, fish and generally play in. This can be accessible via a tap and hose or sprinkler, a water butt, a paddling pool or a special water feature such as a bubble fountain. Watering cans, buckets and a range of water trays are essential.

Resourcing the outdoor environment

Certain children with vivid imaginations will need very little to make their games come alive and become real adventurers. Others will need sensitive support and intervention from practitioners who provide just the right object at just the right time to ensure that the adventure continues.

Conveniently placed storage of 'loose parts' can transform even the most barren environment. For example, near the water zone the provision of pipes, tubing, gutters and a variety of containers or near the construction zone a store with wheelbarrows, blocks, planks, ladders, crates etc. For dramatic areas fabric pieces, cushions, rugs and a variety of different-sized clips and pegs as well as some loose costumes and masks would prove helpful. Such resources are 'loose parts' on which the children can build and adapt. Thus they can find tape to connect gutters, rope to create a den or cardboard tubes to act as telescopes in dramatic play zones. Practitioners can set the children's ideas on fire by also providing provocations or catalysts to challenge them still further on their adventurous journeys. A barrow load of sand on a tarpaulin with a watering can develop play in the construction zone or back packs, maps and a message can add real developmental scope in the dramatic zone. Adapt what you have and use it differently and creatively. Big blocks, canvas, rope and wood can be used in a huge variety of ways as can logs, stumps, gravel and small boulders to create new riskier challenges and opportunities.

It is important to ensure that one particular group does not dominate outdoor play especially with equipment such as bikes where boys and sometimes older/larger girls are inclined to get the 'best bikes' due to their status and size over younger children. It is best not to have bikes/wheeled toys out all the time but use them in relation to particular focus areas of interest and link them to giant sand timers to ensure some fairness of access. The connection between high status equipment and high child self-esteem is important as it has been shown that staff planning and involvement in bike play ensures equity across gender and age. Sometimes the visibility of a practitioner is enough to ensure access for all so that the 'invisible' children can quietly join in without any particular fuss or attention. Equally this can be achieved through some timetabling of areas and resources. You can help this by keeping lists of those involved in such activities such as cookery, woodwork, computer use and going out on expeditions so that all children get the opportunity to be involved. With any limited piece of equipment giant sand timers are very effective and help children maintain equity themselves as well as gain an understanding of the passage of time.

Exciting joint control play can be achieved through garden equipment such as the garden hose. This can be controlled by adults or children to create waterfalls, pools, rivers and lakes for small role-play, paddling or generally having fun getting wet on very hot days. Even shy children when given the hose can show a much more devilish side to their character!

Equipment such as big blocks, tyres, planks, ladders and crates can be used alone or be linked to climbing apparatus such as A frames. These can create amazing structures, dens and imaginary role-play scenarios with very little adult involvement once the children are confident in handling them. Similarly obstacle courses where the height or degree of challenge extends through careful adult observation will keep children growing their confidence and physical skills for long periods of time.

Gardening and similar environmental opportunities outside

Gardening is an essential outdoor experience for young children and can take place in very restricted sites using a wide variety of containers.

The lasting value of gardening goes beyond physicality and being outdoors. It includes areas of learning such as knowing where your food comes from and aspects of healthy living. Research suggests that gardening can help children to become more responsible and calms their behaviour. The manifesto of Learning Outside the Classroom (LOTC) sums the positive view very neatly:

> These, often the most memorable learning experiences, help us to make sense of the world around us by making links between feelings and learning. They stay with us into adulthood and affect behaviour, lifestyle and work. They influence our values and the decisions we make. They allow us to transfer learning experienced outside to the classroom and vice versa.
>
> Teachers.org (2009)

Linked to gardening is a general awareness that young children gain when interacting with an unpredictable environment together with learning about recycling, composting and the nurture of plants both to eat and to enjoy aesthetically. Ann Watts (2011) in her excellent book *Every Nursery Needs a Garden* provides clear guidance on the benefits and concerns plus the designing, planting, teaching and involving young children in a garden.

It is worth developing sensory aspects to your garden however small it may be. A range of containers can form a small garden and features such as a bird bath are all achievable. Sensory gardens are not just to stimulate but also to provide peace and reflection so a small corner with climbing and rambling plants in containers, a seat or bench, wind chimes or a statue, bird feeders and stones can add a spiritual quality. Eco-features can also be built in. It is important to consider ongoing care and upkeep so be realistic about funding before you start. Children will also need proper tools to garden with that are of good quality and appropriate scale for the task.

I have come to experience over the years the 'magic' that sometimes occurs outside where children who have English as an additional language who recognise a vegetable or fruit in the garden that they eat at home or the children who are shy, unable or unwilling for a variety of reasons start to make sense of the world and start to communicate. The outside connects to them and their interests and dispositions in a different way than indoors and the relative freedom and opportunity encourages them to relax and learn more fluidly.

Be aware of dangers

The majority of plants are harmless but children need to learn from an early age that any fruits, seeds, berries, bulbs, roots, stems and leaves of any plant or fungi should not be eaten unless permission is given by a responsible adult. The Royal Society for the Prevention of Accidents produces useful lists of poisonous plants. These are both from the perspectives of being eaten and touched. If you suspect a child has eaten a poisonous plant take the child to hospital immediately with a sample of the plant and a note of the time eaten, quantity and any symptoms. If you suspect skin or eye irritation, wash the area with clean water and seek medical advice again with a sample of the plant.

Environment

Linking the indoor and outdoor environments

> Young children should be outdoors as much as indoors and need a well-designed, well-organised integrated indoor–outdoor environment, preferably with indoors and outdoors available simultaneously.
>
> (Education Scotland 2004)

It is the simultaneous and inter-linked possibilities of the two environments which have so much potential for children's experience of risk, challenge and adventure. It is far more meaningful to the children if the indoors and outdoors have some clear connections. For example, water play on a small scale indoors with trays and pourers and on a much larger scale outside with a large water tray, watering cans and measured beakers. It also allows for in-depth and greater exploration of concepts and skills in different but connected ways. For instance, taking children to a local pond, lake or river once they have already had some experience of different depths of water, how it moves and how things float or swim within it.

In particular practitioners will need to consider the following:

Direct access to and from the outdoor area

There should be easy, daily access to the outdoor area for lengthy periods. A good transition zone between inside and outside with easily accessible clothing, and footwear storage plus matting to stop the worse of mud and damp is important. Such access assists ease of transportation which also makes a huge difference to staff. Adult clothing and footwear should be stored here in order to maximise role-modelling opportunities. Proximity to toilets and hand washing should also be considered.

Special equipment

Although there may be particular resources and pieces of equipment, which are primarily only used indoors or outside, being able to move resources between the two environments can be really empowering and beneficial because it offers open-endedness and flexibility. Certain perishable or high value items will need particular consideration by practitioners to decide if, when and how they will be used so that valuable funding is not wasted. The provision of cheaper, open-ended resources such as cardboard boxes and tyres can help if funds are very restricted.

Cleaning equipment, seating and suitable storage

Whatever the size of space outdoors it needs to be clean, tidy, inspiring and flexible to adults as well as children. Appropriate cleaning tools should be fit for purpose with child-sized versions to encourage children and practitioners to go outside and participate. Seating outside also makes a real difference in widening participation. Storage which is well organised and accessible for children and practitioners is essential if continuous provision is to work properly.

Continuous free-flow play

This is central to quality outdoor play and learning. The mentality of 'play times' will not ensure quality but merely create a temporary respite outside and will not help attitudinal change on the part of those practitioners and/or parents who only see outdoors as a break from proper work in the classroom. Free-flow outdoor play will give both children and practitioners the time to engage deeply, make proper choices for satisfying learning to occur throughout each day, week and year. If there are a wide range of ages accessing the site free-flow play rather than timetabled play, it will generally mean that fewer children will be outside at any one time.

Conclusion

The environment plays a crucial role in enabling children to experience risk, challenge and adventure. This is particularly true for the outdoor environment as children have greater freedom, flexibility and control over their play and learning. Some learning can only really happen outside especially gross-motor development as children can be physically active in a way that isn't possible indoors. The environment should be carefully planned and resourced to ensure opportunities for all children. Learning is enhanced if the indoor and outdoor environments work together and allow for free-flow play. The value of playing and learning outdoors can be maximised if all parties understand these benefits and understand how inside and outside work together. Environments can vary enormously, but any outdoor space even if it is very small can support adventurous play if we as practitioners value it. This potential is only confined by the limits of our imaginations.

CHAPTER 7

Risk assessment

Introduction

Risk assessment is a very large area as it covers innumerable circumstances, environments, transportation, individuals and resources in all sorts of weather. There are no easy quick ways of carrying out risk assessments and any 'off the shelf' methods could be potentially dangerous. This chapter therefore focuses on strategies and ideas to help develop and build practitioner knowledge and practice. It explains such commonly used terms such as risk, hazard, danger and safety. It also aims to clarify adult responsibilities and explain good practice in risk assessment to help create a positive climate for young children to grow up in. As society starts to understand the value of risk-taking, safe practice, positive rules and rigorous risk assessment, a positive climate which nurtures and extends adventure, risk and challenge will emerge and prosper. Risk-taking is often a matter of negotiation with families. It can and should include children, practitioners and local society. If adults locally feel involved in the practical surveillance and protection of children it not only enhances their safety, but also helps to break down distrust and develop community spirit.

What is risk assessment?

Risk assessment is a careful examination of what, in your setting, school or learning environment, could cause harm to people both children and adults. It is a process that allows you to weigh up all the factors which could result in potential harm to individuals. During the process practitioners should carefully consider whether they have taken enough precautions or should do more to prevent harm. Staff, parents and others have a right to be protected from harm caused by a failure to take reasonable control measures.

Clearly accidents and ill health can ruin lives and affect the setting if people are unable to work or play, resources are damaged, insurance costs increase or the setting has to go to court. Therefore practitioners are legally required to assess the risks in the workplace and put in place a plan to control them. It should involve simple, clear procedures and plans so that everyone is protected.

Sensible risk assessment is about:

- Ensuring that staff, visitors and most of all children are properly protected.
- Providing overall benefit to the school/setting by balancing benefits and risks, with a focus on reducing real risks or hazards – both those which arise more often and those with serious consequences.
- Enabling creative pedagogy and teaching practices not preventing it.
- Ensuring that those who create risks manage them responsibly and that if they fail in this duty then robust action will follow.
- Enabling everyone to understand that as well as enjoying the right to protection they also have to be responsible themselves.

Sensible risk management **is not** about:

- Creating a totally risk-free society.
- Generating useless paperwork.
- Scaring people by exaggerating or publicising trivial risks.
- Stopping important learning and play activities for children where the risks are managed.
- Reducing protection from risks that cause real harm and suffering.

The principles were adapted from those launched by Bill Callaghan, Chair of the Health and Safety Commission in August 2006.

It is important for a setting to have a consistent and coherent approach to risk assessment and make sure that this is regularly revisited and taught to all new staff as a main part of their professional induction so they are fit to lead and make sound judgements.

What is reasonable risk?

When carrying out a risk assessment the important question is 'what is reasonable?' The courts now take the view that risks and benefits need to be balanced and any prevention measures must take both into consideration. Where there are risks in an activity which are inherent and obvious and people choose to take part, the law takes a common sense position about duty-of-care taking into account a range of factors to reduce adverse outcomes. One such common sense duty-of-care used at Chelsea Open Air is a pre-trial or pre-visit and site check so all possible risks are considered before the children ever carry out the activity whether on site or out in the community.

Practitioners should also be clear in recognising the important difference between risk and hazard. Hazard is anything or anyone who could cause harm. Everything is potentially hazardous but it is the way that you deal with it that matters. Risk is the measure of the possibility that someone might be harmed by a hazard and therefore you need to make a judgement about whether or not damage is likely to occur. So it comes down to being responsible and making a professional judgement of risk–benefit analysis. Risk is also the element in play that facilitates the opportunity to learn vital autonomous life skills needed in adulthood. Exploring the real world on expeditions and visits, meeting new and different role models and coping with everyday situations through hands-on activities allows children to make decisions within a controlled and managed situation. Gleave (2008) stated that if we do not give children these real opportunities we risk them carrying out their own risk-taking behaviours out of our sight.

Practitioners need to think and weigh up the pros and cons by putting the benefits and your fears in context before coming to a decision. For example, a 2 year old wanting to walk on a low wall – our fears/inhibitions are of the child's developing balance – they can do it with courage and joy or with fear transferred from the caring adult and then may as a result be more likely to fall. Practitioners need to keep hazard in perspective and remember a certain level of risk is positive and natural. We have to strike a balance between the child's right and need to play relatively freely and the possibility of them doing serious damage to themselves in doing so.

What is a practitioner's legal responsibility – what do they have to do by law?

Every day in every learning environment the practitioner should carry out a careful visual check of the area (PAT test) including flooring, empty spaces, lighting, access areas, furniture, toys, equipment, resources and permanent fixtures to ensure that they are in good condition. Any workstations or trolleys for computers and televisions should also be checked and all electrical equipment should have an annual portable electrical equipment test with a dated label on it. Regular daily checks should be taken to ensure that sources of heat such as radiators, window restrictors and hot water are all safe too. Particularly care should be given to fire exits to ensure they are clear, unlocked and easy to open from the inside. Natural ventilation and a reasonable room temperature with the means to prevent glare should be considered as a matter of course.

The Health and Safety Executive stresses that outside play and learning is based upon striking the right balance. Striking the right balance means that:

- schools and staff focus on real risks when planning trips/expeditions;
- detailed risk assessments are used for higher risk activities;
- those running trips/expeditions understand their roles, are supported, and are competent to lead or take part in them;
- the real risks are managed during the trip/expedition; and
- learning and play opportunities are experienced to the full.

Striking the right balance does not mean that:
- every detail should be recorded in copious paperwork in order to provide protection for those organising the trip/expedition;
- when planning lower-risk trips/expedition the risk assessment should be responsive;
- mistakes and accidents will not happen; and
- all risks must or can be eliminated.

Parents and carers should expect according to the HSE 'Those running trips/expeditions need to focus on the risks and the benefits to people – not the paperwork.' This means that staff running trips/expeditions should clearly communicate information about the planned activities to colleagues, parents and carers (and children, where appropriate).

This should explain what the precautions are and why they are necessary to ensure that everyone focuses on the important issues.

Staff running outings/trips/expeditions should act responsibly by:

- putting sensible precautions in place, and making sure these work in practice;
- knowing when and how to apply contingency plans where they are necessary;
- listening to and following advice and warnings from others, such as those with local knowledge or specialist expertise.

The key message from the Health and Safety Executive is: 'Well-managed school trips and outdoor activities are great for children. Children won't learn about risk if they're wrapped in cotton wool' (Health and Safety Executive 2011). They feel that such experiences bring the curriculum to life and help children to develop their own understanding of risk awareness which prepares them for life.

When do you need to carry out a risk assessment?

Risk assessment is not a complicated or burdensome task. It is about good practice and procedures and should link to the setting's Health and Safety Policy. The practitioner should carry out an assessment before you do work or any activity which presents a risk of injury or ill-health. Ultimately it is the responsibility of your employer and often early years staff teams develop risk assessments jointly which cover daily activities and resources such as scissor use, painting, glueing, building with blocks which is good practice. Activities such as woodwork, cookery and gardening are likely to need covering in greater depth. Once a set of core risk assessments are agreed they need to be reviewed annually (unless there are major changes) and provided as part of the induction processes for new colleagues.

Specific risk assessments need to be carried out for the following activities and situations:

- all trips and expeditions;
- visitors to the setting/school;
- children or adults with individual needs;
- activities involving tools use which needs specific teaching, e.g. sewing, cooking, woodwork and gardening;
- more challenging activities involving water, fire etc.;
- reasonable precautions for any person with changed circumstances;
- specialist of new equipment;
- 'one off' events and happenings.

Remember, you do not need to do a written risk assessment every time you get the Lego out – you just need to look at the activity and ask yourself:

- Has this thing/person/activity/situation been risk assessed before?
- What has changed since last time?
- Does the child's/children's/practitioner's mood, the weather or time of day make a difference?

What should a risk assessment consider?

Your risk assessment should consider any individual or activity in play, learning or the environment which might cause harm and how and the people who might be affected. It should take into account any existing controls and identify what, if any, further controls are required.

Your assessment should show that:

- a proper check was made;
- all people who might be affected were considered;
- all significant risks have been assessed;
- the precautions are reasonable, and
- the remaining risk is low.

You do not need to include insignificant risks or risks from everyday life unless your work activities increase the chance of harm.

There are innumerable formats and structures available on the Internet and through local authorities for everyday use by practitioners. The most important factor with children is the adult's thinking process: what is going to happen, where it is happening, how it will be handled by adults and who or what may intervene. It is also important to think about less predictable 'what if scenarios'. If the activity or experience involves going offsite a pre-visit is essential. However, even things can change from day to day and hours to hour so it is always important to prepare for basic facilities such as toilets being closed or the bus breaking down.

You should also bear in mind that what is reasonably practical and safe for one group of children on one day may not be right for another group on another day.

An example of an offsite risk assessment

School/Centre Offsite Activities

Assessor:

Date:

Risk Assessment step by step.

Place to be visited:
Potential hazards:
Persons at risk (e.g. children, parents, students, staff, others):
List existing control measures:
Hazards identified not covered or fully controlled above:
Continual monitoring of hazards throughout the visit:

This format can easily be adapted for new activities indoors and out, new equipment, new skills to be taught, external visitors etc.

Practitioners should also be well versed in their setting's crisis management policy and plan for major eventualities as we live in an age of extreme unpredictability. This is beyond the brief of this book but being 'wise before the event' is a crucial strategy for leaders. At Chelsea Open Air we held our annual themed open day as usual only to experience the London bombings on 7 July 2005 the very next day which necessitated closing the school and children's centre down early whilst caring for children whose parents and carers were very delayed by the traumatic events of the day. So the motto must be 'be prepared'.

Who should my risk assessment cover?

Your risk assessment should cover all groups of people who might be harmed by your premises or activities. Think about:

- Staff affected because of risks associated with the particular jobs they do, such as cleaning, repair and maintenance. Contractors and shift-workers may not be familiar with what you do and the controls you have in place.
- New, less experienced and temporary staff. They may lack the understanding, maturity or professional experience to recognise risks. They may not be familiar with your setting's culture and what is and what isn't acceptable.
- Staff/parents/visitors with poor literacy skills as this can affect their ability to read, understand and follow guidance and instructions.
- Expectant or new mothers and their children as they may be more prone to health-related risks.
- Those with disabilities who may need reasonable adjustments to enable them to work/learn or play safely and minimise the risks.
- Other members of the public and groups of people who share your school/setting.

How to risk assess

Risk assessment is a constant ongoing process which requires the vigilance of all adults and the involvement of the children in order to minimise hazards. The Statutory Framework for the Early Years Foundation Stage sets out the legal requirements that all providers must meet. Providers must have a policy and procedures in two circumstances:

- The environment (paragraph 3.63 of the Statutory framework).
- Outings (paragraph 3.64 of the Statutory framework). (An outing is described as any occasion where you leave the premises with at least one child who is usually cared for on the premises. It does not need to be carried out every time providing there is one in place for that type of outing.)

Such policies should cover how and when risk assessments are carried out according to the premises, layout, location, time of day and ages and needs of the children, who is

Risk assessment

involved in assessing risks, what aspects they cover, what records are needed and how these must be kept.

1 Identify the hazards by reading your risk assessment policy and any procedural guidance or instructions. Walk around the site removing possible hazards, observing people, plants, animals, equipment and objects around you carefully in order to anticipate any possible dangers to the children and if required, talking and asking advice of others.

2 Decide who might be harmed and how (especially those with individual needs).

3 Weigh up the risks and decide upon safety measures and equipment (if necessary) so you can remove the hazard or reduce it by choosing a less challenging option.

4 Record your findings simply (usually in a template) and put them into practice in order to show that a proper check has been made, the precautions are reasonable and that others were involved as relevant in the process.

5 Review your assessment and update if required as people, environments and equipment change. Any accidents or near misses should also be factored in.

Most risks are well known in schools and settings and therefore simple measures will prevent injury or harm. Remember that when considering your risk assessment:

● A hazard is anything that may cause harm.
● The risk is the chance, high or low, that somebody could be harmed by these or other hazards, together with a warning of how serious that harm could be.

Encouraging children to assess risk

Children, technically speaking, present a hazard themselves in that they do unexpected things which adults could not have predicted. So before adults shout at them 'STOP!' or 'BE CAREFUL!' think risk-assessment! Children are biologically programmed to take risks and what they need is a vibrant, flexible and open-ended environment to look, feel and explore within. The equipment/resources children explore will include both fixed and moveable features which should be risk assessed by practitioners so that rich inquiry-based play possibilities are possible. Under the Management of Health and Safety at Work Regulations 1999, an employer has a responsibility to ensure that staff and young people/children are not exposed to risk due to:

● lack of experience;
● being unaware of existing or potential risks; and/or
● lack of maturity.

It is therefore sound pedagogical good practice to involve the children in risk assessment so they start to develop a life skill.

This can be achieved with 3- and 4-year-old children upwards by:

● Involving them in discussion of road safety and use of equipment through play-based scenarios, for example bicycles using small role-play figures.
● Helping parents and carers to understand the risks to the children and how these can be explained to them. For example, there have been advertisements on the radio

which have encouraged parents to teach children about personal safeguarding in that their underwear is private to them and not others.

- Using a series of photographs to show new activities, experiences, or equipment giving the children a chance to share their ideas and concerns about positive usage.
- Getting them to draft a few core positive rules rather than a list of negatives.

Remember the law does not expect us to eliminate all risk but if young children are to benefit from the activity, experience, expedition/visit then they should gain some basic concepts of how to stay safe when properly supervised by a competent person. Then the risks are reduced to the lowest level, so far as is reasonably practical.

A case study example of unplanned risk assessment within a play context

Consider a small group of young children finding an unknown toadstool or mushroom outside in the garden. Whilst there are very clear and obvious dangers to an unsupervised child finding such an item, with the practitioner alongside he/she carries out a quick joint risk assessment stressing how children should behave when finding such material. Then exciting play possibilities can develop and can build knowledge, imagination and skills through sustained shared thinking and exploration with books and creative props. The practitioners role is crucial both in ensuring children's safety and in developing possibility thinking and inspiration to explore further challenges which in turn encourage the child's willingness and desire to continue to make sense of the world and learn more. It is through the crucial intervention of the adult with the 'What if?', 'Could we?' and 'How?' questions that their understanding of hazard and risk-taking can develop. The practitioner intervenes appropriately for safety reasons and yet develops their role flexibly to develop the play and learning possibilities from a potentially hazardous situation.

Bringing parents on board

A process of patient negotiation over time with parents may be essential for them to understand the real benefits to their child. Parents often 'learn' with their first child and are more relaxed with those who follow on as they have the experience of trust and understanding. You can communicate and build confidence by involving parents early on from their child's induction in discussing any fears and safety issues. Listen to their concerns and be ready to learn. Avoid saying 'Don't worry!' You are in loco parentis when they are not present so some trust from them is vital. It is worth stressing that practitioners are doing as the law demands, protecting children as far as is *reasonably practical* like a good and caring parent. This is achieved by carrying out a written risk assessment which helps the practitioner consider, reflect and evaluate any potential hazards alongside the beneficial risks. Such assessments should be shared and discussed with parents and carers involved so they can also consider, raise concerns and be aware of possible hazards.

It is important to establish an ethos where families know from the offset that their child needs adventure, risk and challenge to flourish. Explain that most children see risk-taking as positive and the risks children take proportionally depend upon their age, gender, where they live and their cultural/social background. You can also stress that childhood is about gaining independence gradually and learning to make decisions for yourself for a future world that we do not know or recognise and hence taking more risks is a necessary and constructive part of that process. Carefully discussing crucial factors about risk with colleagues and then sharing these with parents can help with this. This may involve parents' participation in some way such as being able to watch DVD material or discuss photographic images when shown on the whiteboard or computer screen. You can also give uncertain parents the chance to talk with parents whose children have already had the experience or provide website or newsletter items describing expedition experiences written by accompanying parents. The aim is to grow a culture where it is accepted that children need to know about and experience risk.

As a staff team you should create an Outdoor Play Policy with practice exemplars and ask parents to give their perspectives. Although no single policy can list all eventualities, strong examples which have been thoroughly discussed give practitioners (and parents) confidence and enable them to do their job wisely and safely. For potentially more hazardous activities such as woodwork, bonfires and expeditions it is advisable to create individual policy/practice and risk assessment documentation.

Over the years I have encountered many nervous and worried parents. Some worry about accidents in the garden or with use of tools or animals. The majority have had concerns about children going outside on expeditions and whether or not their child can cope with public transport, walking, going to the toilet; carry a small backpack containing their lunch. These fears have to be taken seriously and be given quality time and appropriate attention. Showing parents all the procedures and measures we put in place to ensure the best possible outcomes for each and every experience is key to gaining their trust.

Risky play for children under 3

Babies can thrive outside and the outdoors should have a daily place in their lives so they start to understand the concept. Their encounters should include changes in temperature and different wind speeds. Cooler, outdoor air contains more moisture and is easier on the body's airways and immune system than indoor heated air. Being in a carefully designed outdoor play space provides a more relaxed, less crowded alternative. At this non-mobile age the most important piece of play equipment is the practitioner and the environment.

If you observe a 1 year old who has just mastered the skill of walking you can see how determined and motivated they are to get outside and go somewhere. They quickly learn to negotiate steps, slopes, uneven ground and explore equipment such as balls, bikes, buggies and wheelbarrows with increasingly dexterity. We need to realise that very young children are internally motivated to find their own playful adventures or challenges and to take risks regardless of us being there. By the age of 2 toddlers are more physically active than at any other time in their life. Their interest in large motor movements and more mobile people (both child and adult) helps the toddler realise that others have needs and desires as well as the ability to make plans. We can capitalise on their increasing social play, language development and desire for action by starting to teach them about risk assessment.

Figure 7.1 Thriving outside.
Image taken from *The Power of Physical Play* © Siren Films Ltd (2014).

Children under 3 have less experience of the world around them and practitioners will therefore need to consider their particular vulnerabilities due to age, size, mobility and individual needs in their risk assessments. It is well recognised that babies from when they are first born need to have daily opportunities to move freely on their stomach or back in a variety of stimulating, safe spaces, without being constrained for long periods by clothing, etc. They need opportunities to practise reaching for and grasping objects; turning the head towards stimuli; pulling; pushing and playing with other people, objects and toys. Then they need to play crawling games say over cushions or chasing different sized balls which enhance co-ordination skills. As they master the skill of walking and then running, climbing, throwing and exploring, practitioners will need to carefully assess their abilities in terms of risk assessment for each individual.

Ensuring good practice for all children

Every setting must have a practical (and annually reviewed) Health and Safety Policy with daily activity/experience risk assessments for core activities indoors and out. The setting should also ensure it is supported by basic care provision including a good ratio of trained paediatric first aiders as well as staff that understand and are able to provide professional standards of hygiene, child protection and safeguarding. A trained external visits co-ordinator is also excellent practice. Then the setting can start to develop and agree its core policies and documentation which underline its particularly philosophy and daily practice in the provision of adventure, risk and challenge. Once this stage is reached it is important that the staff understand and practice these agreed standards. Experienced staff can act as leaders on expeditions and buddies to new colleagues going outside for the first time so there is friendly advice and guidance available if required. This is to ensure consistency so the basic rules and practices are followed and the same messages are applied. Any alterations to the usual rules need to be properly explained. For example at Chelsea Open Air the adult message to the children was 'up the steps and down the slide' unless we are being mountaineers when ropes will be fixed to the top of the slide to provide a new and different challenge. This changes the usual sequence of play and gives new enjoyment in ways of using the structure and helps the children master new skills. It is also risk assessed separately. Another example is when a group of children with advanced construction skills were allowed to use the big blocks in their play to create a 'scary ladder', manipulating the rules which usually prevent them from building above shoulder height.

A case study of understanding real risk and hazard with 3 and 4 year olds

Sometimes it is only by experiencing the elements for real that children learn and grow. This I experienced with a Spanish child who we had many years ago who was besotted by fire-fighters. We arranged an expedition to the fire station and he continued to be fascinated and his mother was thrilled. Then we held our annual autumn bonfire and he was scared of the real fire and would not come within 50 metres of the small bonfire repeating many times through his tears 'It's dangerous!' over and over again. His mother insisted she took him home. When asked the next day why he was saying this he replied 'My Mummy is scared of burning.' Now reflecting on this experience I see how important it is to understand the risks and use that knowledge to provide a constructive learning opportunity. Now I would have invited the mother to stay and observe our practice in the hope that they both would begin to relax as they understood our main priority was to keep everyone safe whilst teaching the children to not play with fire but respect it. This was about teaching children about life's dangers and creating a firm foundation for future behaviour.

As Hernandez (2010) says, the earlier children face risks and the opportunities they have to identify risks and act appropriately, the more ready they will be to cope with dangerous situations in real life and resolve problems in the future.

Keeping risk in perspective

We may or may not agree with this but it is worth noting that the Royal Society for the Prevention of Accidents (RoSPA) suggested in 2007 that it would be better for the occasional child to fall out of a tree and break their wrist than develop repetitive strain injury from playing computer games. Peter Cornall, the head of leisure safety at the society, said that children would learn 'valuable life-long lessons by scraping knees, grazing elbows and bumping heads and they would realise how they could avoid hurting themselves in future.' Out of the millions of days of activities for children and young people there are only two or three fatalities per year with only one directly related to the activity itself. We can therefore see that trips, visits and activities are comparatively safe. The biggest cause of accidental death to children under the age of 15 is by road traffic accident, according to UK National Statistics (2014).

Curiously, as Stephen Moss points out in 'Natural Childhood', the effects of society trying to make children safer has had the opposite effect. Ironically by far the most dangerous place for a child to be is in the home according to figures from Child Alert:

> Every year, one million children aged 14 or under go to A&E departments: 30,000 with symptoms of poisoning, mostly from domestic cleaning products, and 50,000 with burns or scald.

> Half a million babies and toddlers are injured each year at home, 35,000 from falling down stairs.

> On average, ten children die each year from falling through a window or off a balcony, while house fires cause almost half of all fatal accidents to children.

According to experts in Health and Safety such as Tom Mullarkey OBE, Chief Executive of the Royal Society for the Prevention of Accidents (RoSPA):

> Counter-intuitively, the key to challenging risk aversion among leaders and decision makers is the application of balanced risk assessment. It is only by objective analysis that the benefits and opportunities of an activity can be weighed against their potential to go wrong. Indeed I feel that the terminology should be changed to risk/benefit assessment. For the most part, as previous generations have learnt by experience, it is rare indeed that a well planned exercise leads to accident. It will instead be most likely to bring a sense of enterprise, fun and accomplishment, so vital for maturity, judgement and wellbeing, which must nearly always offset the residual and inevitable risk. Our mantra at RoSPA sums up this approach: We must try to make life as safe as necessary, not as safe as possible.
>
> Royal Society for the Prevention of Accidents (2010)

Conclusion

The skills and learning which develop from such adventurous and challenging activities and varied experiences of play are valuable throughout life as they create a context for learning chosen by the child. This context is new and different to each child and practitioners and parents need to provide spaces, equipment and opportunities which engage and interest young children providing essential opportunities to learn about risk within safer parameters.

Risk assessment underpins the development of quality experience of adventure, risk and challenge for children and young people. It is not to be ignored or avoided but seen as a rigorous and essential process in ensuring children's safety and wellbeing. Practitioners need to understand the differences between hazards and dangers as opposed to the genuine benefits of risks and challenges in daily good practice. The range and types of risk assessment are very varied but the process of carrying out reliable risk assessments are essential as underpinning good practice in adventure, risk and challenge.

CHAPTER 8

Adding adventure through expeditions and visitors

Introduction

This chapter focuses on developing risk, challenge and particularly adventure by taking young children out into their local community on educational visits to explore, make connections and discover things for themselves. It considers the value and benefits of educational visits, how practitioners choose where to take children, what an expedition might look like in practice and how to plan an expedition in terms of what to think about, where to go and what to take. Finally, it investigates the valuable experiences and practicalities of bringing visitors with particular skills, roles and talents into the setting to widen children's horizons and extend their interests and skills.

The values and benefits of educational visits

Schools and settings have taken children outside their boundaries to provide further experience since the times of the pioneers. Susan Isaacs in *The Intellectual Growth of Young Children* (1930: 288–89), describes taking children out on what she termed 'excursions' and 'at all seasons of the year.' Practitioners still do this today to add value to the children's learning.

Children as natural explorers

Children are natural 'little explorers' as Montessori described. The innate curiosity of young children is the starting point for an expedition. They can be involved to a degree in planning the expedition by discussing their interests with a practitioner and where there may be opportunities to extend their learning further by identifying experiences which are likely to be beneficial. An expedition can 'feed' the child's innate interest and drive as Stonehouse (1988: 13) recognises when describing children as 'tireless explorers, discoverers and scientists who spend most of their waking time investigating the world around them.'

Isaacs (1932: 170) recognised the importance of starting locally and looking at community features that engage children's interest and curiosity and what the benefits might be. She remarked upon the children's 'natural interests' in things and people around them – the street, the market, the garden, the railway, the world of plants and animals – as a means to extend their thinking and problem solving skills. She also saw 'excursions' as she called them as a way for children to gain 'some degree of understanding of the world around him since he has to live in it, and to live safely' (1932: 120) linking such environmental education to teaching children about risk and hazard (1932: 113). She also stressed that educational visits should be 'taken at all seasons of the year.'

> The thirst for understanding goes beyond the mere practical safeguarding of bodily survival. It springs from the child's deepest emotional needs, and with the intelligent child a veritable passion. He must know and master the world to make it feel safe.
>
> (Ibid.)

Offering new experiences and extending children's horizons

The expedition itself offers the challenge of going outside into the world, which for some children can be very limited, whilst for others it may be a rich and frequent experience. Children who lack rich experiences in their lives can particularly benefit if they are supported appropriately in facing these new challenges. These children will gain enormous experience from a simple bus journey or time spent looking at how a shop works by exploring the process from delivery to sale.

Case study: theatre visit

A group of confident, dual language 4 year olds went to experience a local children's theatre production in Spanish of some of the insect poetry of Gabriel Garcia Marquez. It was amazing to observe. The group had been engaged in learning a lot about insects and taking them to watch actors being giant insects within a darkened set and speaking the Spanish poetry did not phase any of them regardless of the fact that only four out of the ten spoke Spanish as their first language.

This expedition helped build an understanding of different backgrounds and heritages as well as developing the initial child focused subject matter.

Rich learning opportunities

Expeditions can assist children's appreciation and understanding of their community and locality. They enable them to explore particular areas of the curriculum through discoveries of the built environment, the natural world, museums, galleries and special experiences such as theatre. These environmentally focused visits can inspire creativity as well as developing cross-curricular learning from a very simple starting point in the community.

Case study

A very mixed ability group explored a family of willow wood elephants created in Hyde Park for a short period to illustrate the plight of the Asian elephant. The sheer sizes and proportions of the immovable creatures allowed the children to go under the bellies of the adults and wonder at the numbers in an elephant family and their different sizes. The mathematical hands-on learning led to a large amount of measurement on our return to nursery as well as many drawings and models of both elephant and human families in a variety of media. The parents who joined this expedition were particularly fascinated in how the children related the elephant family to their own.

An expedition can provide a rare chance to experience animals and nature as well as allow the children to start to compare themselves and explore their possible futures. As Brunner (1977: 17) suggests in his spiral curriculum 'Learning should take us somewhere; it should allow us later to go further more easily.' It is therefore an opportunity to provide a child with some basic knowledge, which can later be transformed or extended through follow up activities. This was particularly evident on the expeditions to Leighton House Museum which displays much of the art collected and painted by Lord Leighton but also provides a beautiful tiled Islamic room with a central water pool. Children instantly quietened themselves and calmly settled around the pool, with adult instruction. They sensed intuitively that this was a place to be respectful and reflective. Their ideas about where the tiles covered in camels, date palms and Arabic script came from and the environments in the world where a small pool of water would be precious were humbling.

Children when interacting with people and things in the environment gradually develop a sense of mastery over the environment as well as a feeling of effectiveness. They gain knowledge, skills and practical life experience as expeditions provide a widening sphere of exploration and help them to develop self-competence. The adults hold the skills to enhance learning by valuing and widening children's creative and cultural ideas by extending their social, language, physical and intellectual thinking skills whilst out and about. On most expeditions with young children, the core of learning is based in the strong social element – the interaction of perspectives and relationships between child, parent, carer staff or venue member. There are also unforeseen opportunities which arise along the way which the adults can maximise as and when these occur.

Children and adults learning together

Expeditions allow not only the children to explore and learn but also the adults.

Parents and practitioners are learning alongside the children as well as learning about the children and how they are responding to these new experiences.

Children with individual needs and interests

The benefits are particularly evident in the case of children with individual needs and those who are particularly able or interested in something. For example, an able child who is fascinated by architecture could gain in-depth knowledge, vocabulary and the opportunity to extend his/her drawing skills through a tailored expedition with a supportive keyworker to a local church. Similarly a couple of children with developmental delay but an evident interest in rotation schema could experience rotation on a giant scale by visiting the London or Birmingham Eye. The cost would not be feasible for a large group but for two or three children the interactive quality would be beyond value.

The benefits of expeditions are varied as can be seen from the examples above. Overall they can be summarised as:

- An exploratory approach based in real children's interests and needs.
- Developing curiosity and peer facilitated learning.
- A rich variety of experience and learning adaptable to different places.
- Active participation in a developmentally appropriate manner.
- Creative opportunities to follow different ideas, discuss learning and represent it differently.
- Reinforcing and extending learning which began at home or in the setting.
- Encouraging and involving active parent/carer engagement in learning as well as developing parental partnership.
- Nurturing a sense of high expectation and enjoyment in learning flow.

Curricular considerations

Curriculum should be a central consideration when planning an expedition. Vygotsky (1962) described children as 'apprentices' and stressed the social context of learning as being crucial in helping children to function at a higher level in the zone of proximal development. In expeditions practitioners are often surprised at how well the children cope with the challenges of the adventure presented to them with very little adult modelling and encouragement. The children rise to the challenge of greater expectations and provide rich and interesting theories and reasoning in the communication and drawings out in the field. Exploration of the natural world is akin to Steiner's principles where not only the carefully planned environment was important, but also the experiences offered which would not only develop the mind and body, but also the spirit. In Wilkinson's book (1980: 6) about Steiner, the child is described as 'accepting the environment' and 'drinking it in.' Such acceptance and thirst can certainly be achieved if the right expedition is matched to the right child. Froebel conversely emphasised the importance of language and communication through discussion to allow children to reflect upon the world and the environment. These seem to be essential to the EYFS curriculum and educational visits can be used to advance areas of learning where children's needs are evident. It was Bruner who introduced the concept of 'scaffolding', providing an orderly process way of teaching which is very evident in expeditions. For example, a child describes the thrill of seeing and hearing a fire engine in the street at nursery and plays with a toy fire engine. The practitioners build upon this interest by organising an expedition to meet real fire fighters, climb on board their engine and try out hoses. This expedition is then followed up again at nursery and new ideas explored through drama using garden hoses, a real fire in a fire pit, and a variety of imaginative play, stories and book making.

What constitutes an expedition?

Susan Isaacs describes a range of expeditions including sailing boats, paddling, shopping, picnics, watching building workers, bridge works, gas main repairs, the railway, going to the post office, the bank and the fire station as well as excursions to churches, cathedrals and museums. An expedition is 'a journey into the world outside of the school which provides experience, exploration and interaction with new individuals, resources and opportunities. It must involve elements of reasonable challenge and "safe" risk in order that the individual concerned experiences the "flow" or thrill and realisation of the excitement of learning' (Solly 2002). Expeditions are about real life and a means for young children to travel into the adult world where what is available for learning is endlessly possible in a way that is not practical in the setting.

The setting should have clear policy and procedures in place for taking children outside the boundaries of their usual learning environment. At Chelsea Open Air we coined the word 'expedition' from a children's story called *The Teddy Bear's Great Expedition* by Prue Theobalds (1990). The story book and the word 'expedition' conveys the care, planning, risk, assessment, communication, partnership and organisation required to take such young children outside their relatively safe setting.

Where to take young children and what to consider?

There are so many different places you can take children that it is not feasible to list them all. The starting point should always be based upon observation of the children's interests and needs. Then talk to other practitioners, ask parents and community members for their ideas and local knowledge, look around you and think creatively as to what might work well. It is often the simple practical things which are the most valuable such as standing on a river bridge. Practitioners could consider the following list as starting points for adventures:

- Museums, galleries and public buildings such as libraries, town halls and hospitals.
- Ancient and famous buildings and structures such as bridges, towers, castles and stately homes.
- Shops, supermarkets, outdoor markets, travel agents and banks.
- Sports areas, open spaces, hills, beaches, parks and gardens.
- Environmental and community facilities.
- Unusual features which may link to learning, schema and interests such as wheels, architecture and trains.

Practitioners will need to explore and discuss the venue in person as some places may not be used to young children or the expedition approach. Once a possible expedition is agreed it is recommended that a familiarisation visit by the designated lead practitioner(s) should be set up to consider practical arrangements such as transport, timings, toilets, meals and storage of coats and equipment as well as what the children will actually do and learn. There may also be a chance to arrange for staff at the venue to add their support.

The setting should devise the process of planning expeditions. This can easily be achieved via a staff meeting to create and agree an expeditions policy which outlines the expectations and processes that must put in place before, during and after taking children out as well as procedures for lost children unless covered elsewhere. It should describe the non-negotiable requirements in clear positive language.

Practitioners take children out on expeditions to add value to their learning in the world as well as developing their life skills. This is also why practitioners should rigorously try to instil road and personal safety by stressing each child's role in 'looking after their grown up', hand washing and other self-help skills, alongside the main learning aim of each expedition. 'Learning is a deliberate process and children need to be consciously aware of what they are doing, learning and understanding in order to make cognitive advances' (Bennett et al. 1997: 123).

What an expedition might look like in practice

An expedition may involve going to a local museum to investigate children's interests in a particular topic such as birds. Going to a museum to look at different types of birds as a result of the children feeding them in the nursery garden is far too vast an area – careful reflection is needed to ensure the focus is both manageable within the time and meaningful to the children involved. Without this the group may wander around, possibly be overwhelmed and gain little learning benefit from the experience. A smaller topic looking, for example, at how birds fly will create a focused core to the expedition and provide enough structure to ensure that everyone's learning is satisfied by the experience and it takes place within the time available.

In practice the practitioners will have identified the children's particular interests and seen the possible lines of development and extension through activities in the setting. This might have involved using books, both fiction and non-fiction, the Internet or through practical means such as feeding birds or recording bird visitors at the bird table. In some situations children may have added the excitement of watching birds of prey flying at a display, wildlife park or zoo. At the museum (with some pre-consultation with the curator) it may be possible to examine and handle stuffed birds of different types (including flightless ones) as well as wings. This may then lead to further interest in flight and flying and how birds and aeroplanes stay up in the sky. This could then be extended to a science museum and to learning more about planes and pilots.

An expedition may arise from a stimulus used within the setting/school. For example, we showed the children who were interested in cats a print of the painting *Tiger in a Tropical Storm* by Henri Rousseau, 1891. This led to practitioners taking a small group to the National Gallery to explore the painting by William Hogarth (1742) *The Graham Children* in which four young children are depicted alongside their cat and bird in a cage. The children were encouraged with both paintings to tell their own stories of what they thought was happening before learning the actual detail behind each picture. En route to the gallery we also stopped to explore and draw the lions situated at the foot of Nelson's column. The tiger print, the gallery painting and the lion statues all added more knowledge and interest to the subject of cats, which went on for nearly six weeks.

Adventure: expeditions and visitors

Equally an expedition might involve a small group who are interested in ICT going on a walk to local shops and businesses. This could develop the children's observation skills by looking at cause and effect within a shopping area, for example, finding out that pressing a button will open or close a door. A group investigated a range of ICT in just a few local streets around Chelsea Open Air: traffic lights, automatic doors, tills and cash points, banking ATMs etc. It also included a passing traffic warden who was using a small hand-held computer to record car number plates. He responded very positively to the children's interest in his machine and showed them what he was doing as a result. On their return to nursery they created their own traffic warden recording boxes using junk materials and were quick to ticket any offending wheeled toys for over a week!

Another range of expeditions could arise from a partnership with a local company such as a visit to a local supermarket to learn about how it works from delivery to checkout. We were able to visit a local department store to observe, draw and discuss the rooftop view from their building to extend the children's fascination in the song 'Rooftops of London' from the film *Mary Poppins*.

Taking children and adults out into the community and its many rich sources of stimuli holds a wealth of creative possibilities and inspiration. I once heard Anthony Gormley, the sculptor, liken art galleries and museums to 'laboratories or treasure troves' and how they have a catalyst effect when used carefully with young children. Huge value can also be found in experiences of local community gems such as walks to the corner shop, bakers, the bridge or post office which can inspire new learning.

Planning an educational visit

What to consider

Start with the children's interests and think about what might be viable and which local links would add value to their learning.

Practitioners should ask the following questions:

- Where do I want to take the child/children?
- Who is this expedition for?
- What is practical in the time available?
- What can they learn about?
- Is it developmentally/age appropriate?
- Is it feasible in terms of distance, cost, weather, ratios etc.?
- How long do we need?
- How are we going to get there and back?
- Who will accompany me?
- What experiences can I provide before we go to support and underpin the potential learning benefits?

Having decided where to go based on the observed interests and needs of the child/children the next consideration is who will be involved. There are many off-site visits which young children go on which include large groups. For under-fives small groups of ten or fewer individuals tends to be most successful. This is because the expedition can then be tailored to meet these children's level of interest and stage of learning and development. Practitioners should avoid the influence of 'off the peg' adult themes dominating the expedition which can be offered in places that provide many out of school visits.

When visiting a building there is often a room set aside for school groups but young children can become overwhelmed or even lost amongst large groups of children. With this in mind set aside a corner or specific area for your base where coats and rucksacks can be stored. Many outside venues are not often similarly equipped so establishing a base camp/meeting point is good practice.

Practitioners should:

- Carry out a written external visit risk assessment and consider all high and medium risks with particular care.
- Think carefully about which children you plan to take and whether or not the expedition is developmentally and physically appropriate.
- Take a basic first aid kit wherever you go for cuts, grazes and stings containing contents suggested by the British Red Cross or St John's Ambulance if you have no guidelines from your paediatric first aid course.
- Take essential medications for individual children/adults with clear instructions for use. Ideally these should be in waist body bags near or on the individual.
- Take a whistle and several mobile phones. Children should know to return to base immediately when the whistle blows and this is the first thing you should teach them and practise before going out of the nursery.
- Take a complete register list of the children and adults with essential/emergency contact phone numbers.
- Keep all play near water very well supervised.
- Remind children to look after each other and the grown ups, to stay together as a group and not to talk to strangers unless with a practitioner.
- Get the children to practise staying together with their adult (practitioner or parent) and not becoming separated. Teach them what to do if they are lost.
- Stress the need not to eat any food, fruit, seeds, nuts or plants unless told they can do so by their practitioner.
- In very busy or vast venues use special identification jackets or ribbons.

Where and when to go

It is a sound rule to stay local as far as possible on expeditions. It will be far more meaningful to the children and families, it saves money and avoids children falling asleep or being ill on long coach/bus journeys. Look around you on your journey to your work place, talk to colleagues/parents who live locally and explore the Internet to find possible places of local interest for the children.

Practitioners will also need to consider the length of the visit. This will be defined by performances/opening times, the setting day and what is achievable within the time period for that particular group of children. If the setting regularly plans visits out there

Figure 8.1 Visit to the river.
Image taken from *The Power of Physical Play* © Siren Films Ltd (2014).

is far less pressure to extend the expedition beyond what is really manageable for the children. The length of the visit will ultimately depend upon the children's level of concentration and the opportunities available which interest them. Never forget that taking children outside is also hard work for the adults involved so it is best to leave when the learning is starting to wane rather when everyone is exhausted and too tired to walk to the bus stop.

What to take

Each child should have appropriate footwear, headgear and clothing for the weather and expedition. If the expedition is for a full day check the children and adults have suitable food and drink in an easily carried rucksack. It is a good idea to have spare rucksacks and suitable weather-proof clothing (including some for parents and practitioners), as inevitably someone will forget theirs.

Otherwise ensure that the following are taken with you:

- Spare clothing including underwear for the unforeseen accident such as sitting in duck poo on the grass.
- First aid kit even if the venue has one as someone may stumble en route.
- Refreshments including water and plastic cups for those who forget or in case someone become over heated or unwell.
- Hand wipes or hand wash for all of the above eventualities as well as before eating.
- An adventure pack of paper, pencils, bug magnifiers etc. This should be customised to the expedition but drawing does help children retain their own view of an aspect of the experience.

- Use a camera or DVD recorder to revisit the expedition for further learning back at the nursery.
- Two mobile phones and detailed child/adult contact list in case one doesn't work or someone has to take a child back due to illness, emergency or similar.
- Money for adult fares and emergencies.
- In some situations beanbags, quoits and a groundsheet may be valuable additions.

Involving parents

It is difficult to over-estimate the excitement for some children and adults when going out on an expedition, and equally true in a few cases, the levels of anxiety. Many parents are keen to accompany expeditions and it is worth spending time with them explaining the school/setting's philosophy and practice with regard to taking children outside into the community. This can both empower parents to understand the great learning potential as well as be willing to take on a role as a helper/chaperone whilst understanding the responsibilities of being involved. It is also helpful to explain how the learning from an expedition can be followed up by the setting and at home through a photo book or further outings led by the parents with their child in their own time. For parents accompanying the children, taking younger siblings is generally not viable or practical as the chaperones will need to concentrate on the children in their care and chasing a toddler or changing a baby's nappy are bound to occur at just the wrong moment. Although parents can find this hard they should appreciate that expeditions are educational visits. Practitioners leading expeditions should encourage parents and carers to share their concerns and issues as these may increase otherwise. If a parent has a real desire to be involved they can sometimes arrange to leave the younger sibling with a relative or friend. Although not legally essential it is also good practice to offer all parents the chance to be police checked for safeguarding purposes so that they can regularly help as accompanying adults on different expeditions.

All parents whose children are going on an expedition will need a letter based upon the information gathered at the familiarisation visit. The letter should be clear and positive including the following:

- Description of the intended expedition and its learning intentions.
- The date and times.
- Ratio of adults to children.
- Mode of transport.
- Food, drink and clothing requirements.
- Any costs.

It is also practical to include a return slip for signed permission and for parents to indicate that they are willing to assist as a chaperone. General permission slips can be created for regular walks nearby to reduce administration.

Ratios should be considered within the risk assessment completed after the familiarisation visit and depend upon the nature of the children. A ratio of 1:2 enhances children's learning experiences but there are a few children with individual needs who benefit from 1:1. The most successful expeditions are for small groups of between four

Adventure: expeditions and visitors

and ten children at a time. By keeping a list and rotating children you can ensure that they all experience expeditions that are suited to them as individuals throughout the year. Staff discussion will identify the children's favoured learning styles, friendships, interests and needs in order to decide on suitable groups.

It is useful to have a short briefing for all helpers/chaperones on an expedition whilst the children are getting ready by going to the toilet and putting on coats and bags. The briefing should summarise:

- Where the expedition is going.
- How the group will reach the venue and anything to note about public transport.
- What facilities are available including toilets for adults.
- Double-checking that the adults have their lunch, a drink, emergency money, travel card or fare if applicable.
- The sorts of things the children will be doing and how these can be supported and extended.
- Ways to encourage positive behaviour, avoid losing children and what to do in the case of unforeseen events.
- Examples of responses by children and how to extend their learning using open-ended questions and comments.
- What happens on the return to the school/setting.
- Giving time for other questions.

Chris Parsons (1995: 16–18) suggests many ways to involve families on what he calls 'a joint learning adventure'. These adventures were particularly aimed at museums where it was found that parents leading groups of children used a social interaction style similar to that of a family visiting a museum. In comparison teacher-led groups used more formal 'chalk and talk' approaches based upon the material to be learnt. The parent chaperones relied on information signs, museum guides and joint exploration with their charges which in turn led to 'relationship building'. The only difference between family groups and parent-chaperoned groups was their lack of 'history', having not visited the museum before. Falk and Dierking (1992) identified this shared or 'joint memory' as being retained for 15–20 years.

As expeditions take different children to different places parents can perceive that there is some inequality occurring. Again practitioners need to prepare parents so that they understand that all the children will go out at one time or another but to different places and for different reasons. Practitioners are crucial in fine-tuning the planning in order to raise achievement as well as scaffolding the expedition to support and extend the play and learning for particular individuals and groups. It is also wise to explain to families that children need to be well settled before going out on expeditions. This gives practitioners time to get to know them and provide a suitable expedition for their child.

The expedition environment is not in itself the teacher, but merely the catalyst or enabling structure which helps practitioners and parents realise the aims and intentions for children's learning (and sometimes their own too). Guy Claxton (1990) states, 'learning always involves a modification of what you already believe or know.' If the children (and indirectly practitioners and parents) are given new challenges and opportunities to 'struggle' (pedagogically speaking) on expeditions they will rise to the challenge, adapt, problem solve and build upon previous learning.

Bringing visitors into the setting

The other area of stimulation and extension for learning in the early years are visitors. Visitors widen the background, heritage, gender and ethnicity role models available to young children. They can provide superb opportunities for the children to learn about their lives and work, interests and hobbies. These visitors can build children's sense of self-worth and confidence as well as their understanding of the local community and wider society and respect for society's diversity. Their visits are not ad hoc but, like expeditions, should be planned to link and extend the children's interests, needs and add value to the pattern of the year. They include those who help us such as the mayor, a hairdresser, a police officer or an orthopaedic surgeon to visitors with particular skills, experiences, disabilities and hobbies such as a violin maker, pensioner, the blind storyteller, the grandma who crochets or a local artist. They can include bathing a baby sibling or a walk down the road to meet a police horse or a crane driver before watching him operate the crane at a distance.

The benefits of bringing visitors into the setting include:

- Forming positive relationships.
- Building awareness of the contribution different people make in their work and community roles.
- Learning anti-discriminatory attitudes from different role models.
- Building an understanding of their own and others' cultures.
- Building a sense of community and fostering a sense of belonging.
- Beginning to develop respect, politeness, interest, appreciation, empathy and sensitivity to others and their needs.
- Beginning to ask appropriate questions of a stranger and listen to the answer.
- Engage in conversation and learn to listen to less familiar voices.
- Start to see things from another point of view.

Curriculum benefits

The curricular gains are clear. Communication and language can benefit richly from these real reasons for talking and listening. They can later back at the setting be linked to literacy- and numeracy-related activities such as early writing, calculation and recording. There are also clear curricular links to Personal, Social and Emotional Development in terms of making relationships, behaviour and self-control as well as fostering self-esteem and gaining opportunities to flourish. There are many obvious aspects of Understanding the World in learning about their community and locality. Physical Development can be underpinned by learning about personal safety, road safety and hygiene and through meeting medical and care visitors. Others will inspire children to be physically active by running, climbing and playing football. Dancers, poets, artists, drama productions, musicians and sculptors can nurture the Expressive Arts.

Working with visitors to the setting

The visitor should be supported by at least one staff member working with small mixed ability/age groups throughout the day. This enables the children to concentrate and engage effectively and avoids overwhelming the visitor who may not be familiar with the learning and development needs of young children. Practitioners then get the opportunity to observe and record the children interacting with another adult or participating in a new experience and then further extend their own learning about the children through follow-up activities.

Practical tips when involving visitors

To ensure safe and developmentally appropriate practice the following should be considered when planning to involve visitors:

- Draft a clear statement or policy as a setting/school which underpins your practice for involving visitors in learning.
- Establish systems for safeguarding frequent visitors and supervision for 'one-off' visitors.
- Inform parents about the visit.
- Agree which staff will make the initial contact.
- Arrange a familiarisation visit to discuss how the visitor can support the children's learning, interests and needs.
- Discuss appropriate language and questions.
- Plan the date, time and duration of the visit.
- Agree the space and any equipment plus any risk assessment requirements.

Staff responsibilities with visitors

Good practice should involve the following:

- Planning ahead and arranging visitors for particular events and festivals well in advance linked to the yearly plan.
- Welcome, support and thank the visitor.
- Ensure security, supervision and safeguarding procedures are followed at all times.
- Act as an enthusiastic role model in responding to the visitor for the children.
- Offer the visitor refreshments and comfort breaks.
- Take charge of any health and safety issues through a risk assessment as well as behaviour management.
- Carry out follow up arrangements including thank you letters, paying invoices and informing families of the value of the visit through observations, displays and newsletter/website write-ups.

Summary

Expeditions and visitors are about real life interactions for young children. There are many benefits for the children if their practitioners are thorough in their planning, preparation and execution of these educational opportunities. These enhance positive feelings as well as more concrete learning. The experiences gained on expeditions and from visitors go beyond the value of routine education as they give children the chance to enjoy and participate in learning about life.

CHAPTER 9

Dealing with concerns

Introduction

Different people have different views of adventure, risk and challenge. In this chapter the views of children, parents/carers and practitioners are the main focus as they are of the greatest importance and need to be taken seriously. The chapter looks at what the particular concerns are for parents, practitioners and children. It considers where these concerns may originate from and what we can realistically do to overcome them to ensure the ongoing positive learning experience of young children. Finally, it looks at the most common concerns and how these might be practically addressed.

Background to parental concerns

The concerns and worries of parents are individual due to their uniqueness and the uniqueness of each child. Concerns can be numerous and taken seriously because fear of various hazards may impact upon children by limiting their play and learning.

For many parents rearing children in the 1950s and 60s, adventurous play involving risks and challenges would have been natural. However, a parent then was far more likely to be at home or working nearby and available to help if the child needed them. Society's view of outdoor play has changed radically since those days, resulting now in a media maelstrom when a terrible accident happens to a child or young person through any outdoor activity. This can lead parents to believe that the world is set on killing their child and they must keep them well away from such potential harm. Family life has also changed dramatically. Children's 'radius of activity' (the size of the area around their home where they are allowed to roam) has reduced significantly since the 1970s. Playing out in the street or park is no longer the norm for many children due to parental fears and society's perception of child rearing.

Every new parent starts to worry before a baby is even born. The enormity of dealing with their fears once the child is old enough to leave the family home, play with other children and learn from a wider range of adults can be hugely stressful. This is normal and as each child and family is unique their fears will vary greatly.

Lack of experience often causes new parental uncertainty and parents can be persuaded by friends, the media and professionals that only safe and limited play is feasible for their child/children. Parents who have had dealings with social care professionals may be very cautious and sometimes over reactive in their questioning about the cause of every bruise or scrape at nursery so that their parenting is not brought into question. These adult worries can transfer directly or indirectly to the child making them fearful, shy or reticent to participate. Young children know intuitively when their important adults are fearful. 'A happy child is a child who will learn' is a phrase often used in the early years but a happy child needs a happy parent to gradually let go of the apron strings.

There are many reasons why parents may not want their child to participate in what they see as dangerous activities and experiences. These may result from their own experiences and how they were reared, their culture, religion, gender or lack of familiarity with how education and care is provided in the UK. Understanding the parent's previous experiences, recent changes in the home context such as bereavements and their own educational experiences will build a foundation for practitioner empathy. A parent who is recently separated or whose partner is in prison may have very evident reasons for not trusting their child to another adult. Some parents will be wary of risky play because they were injured as a child or educated abroad in a very formal context and expect the same for their child. Others will want very different experiences for their child to their own upbringing. Families may have escaped as refugees or asylum seekers losing virtually everything and therefore their child is even more precious. This can also be true of children where they have resulted from such circumstances as IVF, difficult pregnancies, been seriously ill, premature or had challenging births. It is also true of those with special educational needs as there can be a perception that they need to be kept protected and safe from harm. In these contexts it is totally understandable for a parent to be more worried. It takes the professional skill and patience of the practitioner to gradually support the parent's confidence in their child's right to experience safe risks and challenges within a well planned, risk assessed environment alongside well trained staff.

There are also some fears, which cannot be explained. These may stem from separation, divorce, domestic violence or mental illness. For a few parents the desire for their child to be successful may lead to an overactive pursuit of enrichment activities resulting in the child being at a loss when left to their own devices and potentially getting into serious danger because of this.

How to support parental concerns

Many parents can be reassured when practitioners take the time to explain how children learn and how the setting's policies and procedures support children's safety, happiness, learning and wellbeing. A succinct and clear explanation in relation to their child of the learning benefits of risky play and why certain challenges and adventurous opportunities are on offer will go a long way in supporting parental understanding. There also needs to be time and respect for individual questions and time to consider new concepts because these will have different ramifications for each child. This does not mean practitioners promising that there will be no accidents but rather providing clarity about what happens if a child has an accident or the measures taken to risk assess the site and resources before the children enter each day.

Dealing with concerns

The process of changing minds is gradual. As the parent becomes confident and more relaxed then so too does the child. This leads to the practitioner feeling more self-assured as part of this three-way relationship. Once the child is confident practitioners can further enhance the relationship by showing the parents photographs or DVD material of their child climbing trees or doing whatever the parent is fearful of. Very often the first thing parents say is 'they might fall' whereas practitioners might say – 'Look at how well Freya is climbing and balancing.'

As the parent/practitioner relationship develops parents will start to discuss, learn more, understand and value the genuine opportunities of risky play and challenging learning. Clear and ongoing communication is essential and settings should make their expectations clear around considerations such as clothing and footwear as sometimes these get forgotten and lead to hazards for the child. Settings need to share their policies and procedures about how they use resources, the weather and how natural play experiences such as rough and tumble play are provided. They also need to share how more challenging activities such as water play, woodwork, animal handling and fire are dealt with. This can be through displays, observation, newsletters and the website. Clearly explaining what is happening each week, when it is happening, what is expected and why and the relevance to the children's learning and development will be very reassuring for parents.

The specific concerns of parents and how to deal with them

Strangers

'Stranger danger' is high on the list of parental fears. We are hard wired to fear strangers. As Richard Louv points out, the 'bogeyman syndrome' (Louv 2005: 123) may actually be counter productive today as the greatest danger to children is not outside in the woods, fields and parks but at home as the majority of abuse is carried out by relatives or close friends of the victim or via the Internet. Parents need to feel confident in the safeguarding and vetting procedures in their child's setting by having them explained and practitioners demonstrating how they work if necessary. They need to understand how their child is kept safe and secure in terms of appointments and visitors through the use of visitor check-in procedures, badges and door security for everyone entering and exiting the premises.

Getting dirty

This is a very practical concern and particularly affects families where poverty or limited resources are an issue. Practitioners need to explain to parents that their children will get dirty by playing but encourage them to provide older clothes as well as aprons and outer gear to prevent the worst damage. The provision of a washing machine and dryer is essential as then the situation can generally be rectified before the child goes home. For special occasions and events it is advisable that parents bring in clothes for children to change into after the session has finished. Equally it helps parents if the setting is having photographs taken of the children for staff to avoid 'messy' activities that day to avoid damaging special clothes.

Physical safety

First and foremost, children need to feel safe. If their parents are worried about them this anxiety transfers and results in a less confident child who may be reluctant to join in. There is a hierarchy of 'feeling safe,' the most fundamental level of which is physical safety. Parents need to know that their child is free not only from physical harm in terms of the environment and its resourcing but also from forms of verbal/social aggression, be it bullying or emotional threats. Understandably parents (and practitioners) are first and foremost focused on issues of physical safety. These fears can be addressed by sharing the basic rules of the setting and the policies and procedures which provide a firm foundation for safety and wellbeing such as those around behavior and discipline, first aid, crises management and health and safety. Practitioners also need to know the skills each child starts with. During induction parents should be encouraged to share their child's abilities and skills as well as areas they need to develop particularly those the parent is worried about. Whilst most children will not over reach themselves, a few children with unique needs may have no real sense of danger and need careful one-to-one supervision from their very first day. During induction parents can to be encouraged to share their child's experiences at home and in the world around them. This will help practitioners prepare environments that build on familiar experiences at home rather than outright challenge from the start.

Illness

Some parents may find rules about illness difficult particularly if they are working and are some distance away. Any rules should be central to the rights of the child (as well as all the other children) and if unwell they need to be with their loved ones. The setting should ensure families understand their obligation to collect their child and have up-to-date contact numbers for parents/carers as well as at least two other reliable and familiar contacts who can collect the child if necessary. These contacts can of course be used in the case of accidents too. Sometimes families will flout these expectations and will need reminding that they are impacting on the rights of other children, families and the staff themselves. In the case of a severe accident a senior staff member should accompany the child to hospital in an ambulance and stay with them in loco parentis whilst other senior staff contact the parents so they can understand what has happened and arrive to look after their child.

Background to practitioners' concerns

The role of practitioners as boundary setters or 'gate keepers' in children's use of outdoor spaces has been widely discussed particularly in relation to the influence of parental fears and anxieties on children's physical skills and the likelihood of accidents. Research suggests that, in line with Tandy's (1999) findings, children's use of outdoor space reflects

Dealing with concerns

the ways in which they negotiate their own desires alongside 'parental constraints'. To gain maximum benefit from outdoors a child needs to have their parents' support and understanding. This sometimes means that the practitioner is left in the middle trying to do what is best for the child's health, wellbeing, learning and development whilst not wishing to antagonise parental wishes.

Dealing with specific practitioner concerns

Fulfilling curriculum requirements

Practitioners have to fulfil the requirements of the EYFS by providing a rich array of experiences and activities inside and out. However, the constant and rapid change of the expectations placed upon them leaves some feeling unsure and unsupported as to how best to provide these in the very variable contexts in which they work. Practitioners need to use their rich knowledge of child development and the principles of the EYFS as the basis to all they do. Through close observation of young children's interests during their child-initiated play they have the best starting point to provide high quality pedagogy that makes a real difference to children's learning and progress.

Safety and fear of legal action

Today practitioners can cite their fear of inspection by Ofsted as a reason not to take children outside. Health and safety legislation has sometimes been misinterpreted because there are fears that firstly something dreadful may happen and secondly that they will be held to account. Any practitioner who plans learning around the children's interests and knowledge and carries out the policies, procedures and risk assessments of their setting fully has nothing to fear from the law. This is because the practitioner is acting as a good and caring parent would to ensure the health, safety and wellbeing of the child. It should be remembered that each child is unique and in some individual cases, particularly with children with special educational needs, a slow step-by-step strategic approach will highlight any areas of concern or areas which need adaptation for reasons of health, safety and wellbeing. Occasionally practitioners will need to have the courage of their convictions and follow their intuition – again carefully but positively. High quality training and professional development is crucial as it provides a tapestry of ideas, resources and practices to use and adapt daily. Ultimately practitioners need to be brave and try!

Safety is an interesting concept which practitioners need to consider in relation to risk. Protecting children and trying to keep them safe from injury is a mistaken view because the real world is full of risks – physical, social, emotional, intellectual and financial. However, reasonable risk is essential for the healthy development and lifelong learning of all children.

Practitioners need to strike a balance between the risks and benefits of outdoor, risky and challenging play. This decision should be based upon policies, risk assessment and what a good and caring parent would do. There is a trade off between safety and risk benefit. Offering opportunities for risk, challenge and adventure which have been suitably risk assessed and considered as purposeful by the setting is far safer than children seeking out those not designed for them in places which are far from ideal and may lead to serious harm. Purpose designed activities and experiences for play and learning indoors and out are generally less likely to incur litigation issues.

Ratios

Ratios are a concern for practitioners because a reasonable adult to child ratio has been shown to aid the quality of provision when balanced to the ages and stages of the children's development and needs. This must be carefully tailored to the circumstances by ensuring that students and newly qualified staff are not left alone but adequately supervised inside and out for the safety of the children and themselves. However, there may be lots of practitioners within an area but inadequate provision. All the practitioners need to properly understand their roles and responsibilities. Quality provision means moving around observing and engaging with different groups of children in their play at teachable moments to extend and enhance their learning rather than simply keeping an eye on behaviour. Ratios help those who fear litigation by providing adequate adult supervision to the experiences being provided. Practitioners can find working outside more challenging due to the space and more varied choices available to the children. Outside can therefore be perceived as needing a higher ratio of adults so that practitioners can maintain safety and ensure quality play and learning are being provided. In fact the reverse is true as when practitioners involve themselves in the children's interests the children concentrate and play far more effectively.

There should always be practitioners available indoors and out so that the children always have access to teaching and support. Ideally outside this should be at least two staff so that one practitioner can engage in specific activities whilst the other moves around supporting and extending children's play and learning more generally.

If you ask early years settings about ratios outside a wide range will be quoted: 1:3, 1:6, 1:13 and so on. The ratio is not really the issue but practitioner knowledge, confidence and expertise are. If practitioners believe that children benefit from being outdoors then risky and challenging experiences will be provided and in most cases will have similar ratios to indoors. However, if the site is more challenging and if children with disabilities and special educational needs are involved then staffing ratios must be higher.

Leadership

Leadership is crucial in setting an example. If the leadership team doesn't go outside and learn alongside the children there will be little desire for anyone else to take it on. There has to be a clear understanding and foundation of training for practitioners when developing outdoor play and learning so that a culture of adventure, risk and challenge develops steadily and that the practitioners themselves feel able to rise to challenges. When joining a setting, practitioners will need time to fully understand the ethos, principles and vision as well as gaining a basic idea of how the setting works in practice before they start work. There may be also staff with very individual fears such as spiders, snails or in my case spiral staircases! These are all surmountable in that one can value a

Dealing with concerns

spider and the child's fascination without touching it, whilst other colleagues can take one's place in going up and down the staircase.

Induction procedures for practitioners should be underpinned by training in health and safety, safeguarding, risk assessment and first aid as well as any specific activities and experiences such as woodwork, bonfires, animals or expeditions.

First aid, illness and accidents

There should be an adequate number of paediatric first aiders on site and out on expeditions. All practitioners need to be aware of who the first aiders are. All staff should be very clear on the basics of what to do in the case of minor and more serious accidents and be encouraged to keep calm if possible. Not everyone can be a natural at first aid so those who are not trained are far better distracting and occupying the other children whilst the trained first aider manages the situation and decides if further external medical help and parents are required. Each setting will have its own policy and procedures in place but these should include written advice to parents of all minor accidents which they read, understand and sign off so that should a child be taken ill later they can inform the medics.

Practitioners will also need to be sensitive to the views of parents with regard to risky play. They should explain daily activities to interested/concerned parents particularly during the early days when the child is settling in. Any accidents and behaviours should be fed back calmly in a non-judgemental style avoiding names so that parents understand what is going on but do not get upset or angry. If the circumstances are particularly sensitive and delicate, withdrawing into a meeting room with some privacy is advisable.

Suitable clothing

No one likes to be cold and wet through or too hot. Staff should be provided with some basic clothing and equipment to suit the weather. This should include warm, waterproof gear as well as sun hats and cream. At a practical level the flexibility of the team to allow colleagues to change over from outside to in during extreme weather to warm up or cool down is equally important. Dangerous weather such as thunderstorms and very high winds should bring everyone indoors regardless.

Daily safety procedures

Staff will need inducting into a daily check of the site and any equipment and resources they are using as these can deteriorate or fail without warning. Their vigilance in removing and reporting such faults can shield the children from real hazards until the faults are either rectified or the equipment replaced. All practitioners should bring such faults to the management's attention as well as completing and sharing incident or near miss/accident reports. This is far healthier and safer for children than leaving faulty equipment hidden at the back of cupboards just waiting for an accident to happen.

Individual needs and considerations

Particular consideration must also be given to the individual needs of those who are pregnant and those with disabilities. This requires good communication as well as developing agreed ways of working that are shared with all practitioners in a climate of mutual support and understanding.

Background to young children's concerns

There is evidence to show that as children age their fears increase, particularly in relation to dangerous strangers. Siblings and playground companions may have an influence on the views of younger children. Children have reported fears of public spaces and natural spaces and have been shown to equate home with 'safety' (Harden 2000). Tandy's (1999) study of Australian children indicated that they preferred to play inside the home. Thomas and Thompson (2004) discuss an increasing reluctance amongst children to play in public spaces due to their fear of traffic accidents. In research on views of woodland, O'Brien (2005a) found that 8 to 10-year-old children have fears of such spaces because of potential encounters with dangerous strangers. There is a general trend for children to view green areas that are close to home as less 'hazardous' (Harden 2000). However, Groves and McNish (2008) show that children have increasing capacity to risk assess effectively when playing outdoors.

Research also highlights a certain gender divide related to the ways in which girls and boys want to use outdoor and public spaces. Differences have been shown in relation to the types of spaces they like and will use and the types of facilities they want to see improved (Roemmich et al. 2007). Studies show that boys enjoy playing further away from their home than girls (Valentine 1997). There is also evidence of different views from different socio-economic backgrounds. Thomas and Thompson (2004) suggest a link between poverty and access to outdoor spaces for children. This may affect young children who are less likely to access 'street play' or to play in parks or recreational facilities due to their age and vulnerability. Despite the above, most young children under 5 see the outside as an area of great possibility – a tapestry in which to weave their ideas and imagination, a place where challenges, adventures and of course all sorts of risk are viable.

Dealing with specific concerns of young children

Lack of appropriate clothing

The provision of purpose-designed outdoor play wear is essential for children's full participation in experiences. If you only have one coat it is only natural that you and most definitely your parents will not want it messy at the end of a session. Likewise shoes. The provision of clothing and wellington boots can be addressed by asking the families with older children who are leaving the setting for any out-grown donations, which can be put towards specific wet/cold weather gear. Waterproof dungarees with separate jackets are far more practical for 3 to 5 year olds as they can be independent in

Dealing with concerns

their hygiene needs as well as using them on warmer days with the hosepipe. Babies and toddlers are better in all-in-one suits.

Family views

Many of the concerns of young children are echoed from overhearing their parents. Sometimes young children can be reticent to go outdoors due to family/cultural views on the effects of, for example, cold, frosty days. Some parents from warmer climates may impose their dislike of the cold upon their child by telling them to stay inside, setting up a real conflict for the child. There may be some children such as refugees and asylum seekers who are naturally fearful of strange places because of their own personal experience. Other children such as travellers may find it far harder to be indoors because of their particular family/cultural heritage and experience. These children and parents need a gentle sensitive approach which allows them choice rather than compulsion so they learn to love both environments and see the huge and exciting possibilities for their own play and learning.

Accidents and getting hurt

If we teach children to ask themselves: 'is it a good idea if I…' they can start to risk assess their own behaviour for themselves. If they are involved in walkabouts around the site and premises they can also learn to identify potential hazards as a routine part of the day. This can lead to lots of discussion about how to stay safe as well as greater understanding and awareness of the world around them.

Practitioners should see themselves as 'enablers' of outdoor and challenging play. The ability of practitioners to model such teaching by using phrases with children such as 'If you hold the ladder now, you will feel safer' and 'You need a lot of practice at climbing to reach the top' or 'Try coming down backwards like James' can really empower them without destroying emerging confidence.

Strangers

Children learn gradually through widening their experience of the world. Like the skills for learning to cross the road, their knowledge and understanding is cumulative and is enhanced by life experience of meeting strangers within safe contexts. Young children learn from their peers and staff in the setting environment and this broadens the picture they have gained in their family context. As the school/setting brings in experiences of different visitors the child's world enlarges. It is important that children understand that there are strange adults in the world who can help them if they are in danger, lost or frightened such as police, ambulance and fire personnel, medical staff and if these aren't available female staff serving in shops or mothers with children in buggies.

Bullying and rough play

Physical roughness and potential bullying often occurs when children are developing their language and social skills. Children who have developing skills in these areas will often use their bodies to communicate their messages by pushing, pulling or snatching. Teaching all children the Makaton or BSL signs for 'Stop it! I don't like it because...' can generate important and clearly understood messages. The other children learn that this is a cornerstone of the 'rules of engagement' and quickly find a practitioner if the child continues the negative behaviour. The practitioners' observation of children and intuition are a good way of picking up mischief. Then by using puppets and role-play, practitioners can diffuse a situation and allow the children to practise and learn more positive behaviours instead.

Making and staying friends

Practitioners need to deal sensitively with children's play and relationships. Children may have difficulty in coping with their feelings and frustrations and coming to terms with similarities and differences when starting to make friendships. This is truer if they are not familiar or comfortable in the environment. If the practitioners engage with children and find out what motivates them their positive behaviours are likely to be imitated as the children copy them as role models and respond with positive behaviours and learning. The nurturing of this social learning develops a type of collective understanding or intelligence as to what the rules of engagement in play and learning area.

Common concerns and how to deal with them

Bare feet

Bare feet will result in a few stubbed toes and broken nails, but generally children can play barefoot without injury and improve their co-ordination, balance and physical development as a direct result. It can also help them develop their skills in dealing with footwear. Putting these benefits to parents against a few dirty pairs of socks is usually very positive.

Clothing

Many adults worry that children have too few clothes on but as the child rushes around they do not feel cold. The issue arises when they stop and are still. Too many layers on can result in children becoming drowsy and dehydrated. The best way is to encourage clothing suited to the weather/season plus one extra layer. Hot sunny weather is often not best served by not wearing T-shirts as young children's skin is delicate and their heads and shoulders need protection from the sun's harmful rays by wearing suitable headgear and tops and applying sunscreen. Suitable clothing can be obtained from a variety of manufacturers, for example Muddyfaces (www.muddyfaces.co.uk).

Dealing with concerns

It is also practical to have a complete change of clothes for children (and adults) on site. Collecting used mittens, gloves, socks, underwear and general clothing for accidents is useful. Socks are great substitute mittens in snowy weather when all the mittens and gloves are cold and wet.

Climbing and sliding

These are fairly standard childhood pursuits but they do have clear hazards. Whilst moveable equipment can be set up at different heights according to the sizes, abilities and ages of the children, fixed equipment and trees cannot. Young children are generally wise about climbing and do not take on a challenge that they do not feel capable of (with the exception of a few children with individual needs). As practitioners we need to consider in our risk assessment not only the child's age, stage of development and height but also if they will need the provision of rubber surfacing or mats around the climbing feature. We should also think about their clothing and footwear when climbing. Lots of good ideas are available from Siren Films (www.sirenfilms.co.uk).

Heights, drops and surfaces

Young children naturally like to balance along walls but adults often feel the need to hold their hand to prevent falls without thinking that they are giving an unspoken message of fear to the child. Practitioners need to stand close by but not intervene. Using a variety of frames, planks, ladders, tyres, crates and similar equipment arranged at different

Figure 9.1 Balancing with adult close by.
Image taken from *The Power of Physical Play* © Siren Films Ltd (2014).

heights and angles, obstacle courses can be created to provide further challenge as the children's confidence and competence increases. If the environment has a range of natural and tactile surfaces outside including boulders, pebbles, granite sets, wooden posts and stepping-stones parents may be concerned about falls and scrapes. It is therefore sensible to explain to parents how the different surfaces benefit children's physical development, balance and co-ordination and provide different sensory experiences.

Tyres, crates and boxes

These are great for low obstacle courses and provide fun, problem solving and challenge if they are used for building or in the case of tyres to bounce down a series of steps or roll down a slope with clear visibility. There can be fears of protruding metal emerging from the rubber, or cracked plastic cutting or trapping fingers so they need to be checked regularly.

Wild animals

If you have wildlife in your outside area, particularly foxes and domestic animals, a separate risk assessment should be carried out. Generally wildlife vanishes when the children arrive on site so a site inspection should be carried out daily before the children arrive to check for visitations. Rodents will need external professional expertise as will larger animals such as foxes and badgers. If you have a bird table you will need to be vigilant with regard to the foodstuffs provided for the birds as some may be allergens or develop mould and fungi. Insects and mini-beasts are often of great interest to young children, who should be encouraged to respect them and treat them with care by leaving them alone unless with an adult. Pond life should be considered separately due to fears of drowning and swallowing dirty water.

Domesticated animals

Working with the RSPCA and becoming an Animal Rights Respecting School can be useful as it prevents all the uncertainty of setting pets and their sometimes variable quality of care during weekends and holidays. Bringing in domesticated animals can be beneficial such as a travelling farm where the animals are used to being handled and are checked regularly for their health and wellbeing. Access to such animals is valuable to children as they learn about the food we eat and how to care for animals. Grooming a pony, bottle feeding a lamb and collecting eggs can be valuable challenges as well as experiences of awe and wonder. Some children will be very scared to start with but will gradually come alongside rabbits, guinea pigs and young ducklings and chicks. Knowing each child helps predict which creatures are more likely to be most suitable for introduction. Whilst there should be an overall risk assessment for such farm visits that considers each creature, there are some children with individual needs who may also need separate risk assessments in order to meet the animals safely. Tarpaulins to cover up any special ground areas before the visit and the effective use of a yard broom, hosepipe and good disinfectant such as Jeyes Fluid after the event are essential.

Dealing with concerns

Practitioners will need to monitor the children and the animals throughout. Children need to avoid putting their fingers in their mouths and should eat well away from the animals. General and specific guidance on farm and domestic animals can be found on the RSPCA website (www.rspca.org.uk/adviceandwelfare) and Department for Environment, Food and Rural Affairs (ahvla.defra.gov.uk/official-vets/Latestnews/news-item6.htm) and specifically for pregnant women: http://homefarmer.co.uk/pregnant-women-advised-avoid-animals-giving-birth/.

Plants

Plants can be potentially hazardous whether wild or grown for food, as young children can be allergic sometimes with life threatening consequences. Watts (2011) provides an excellent starter list of plants to be avoided including aconites, ivy, elderberry, foxglove, laburnum and lupin. Children can, however, learn that picking any plant, fruits, seeds or berries removes food from the animals and can be potentially hazardous for themselves. Forest School expeditions provide children with real opportunities to learn that brambles and holly scratch, nettles sting and so on. Over time children learn to recognise these plants and avoid them. They also learn about the use of dock leaves as nature's remedy for nettle stings! Many seeds and bulbs of plants are poisonous such as apple pips, sweet pea, tulip and daffodil plus rhubarb leaves, uncooked potato tubers, chillies, mushrooms and parts of tomato plants but if the children wear gardening gloves as a matter of course and wash their hands properly afterwards there is little risk. Cacti, holly, ivy and poinsettias at Christmas, conkers and acorns in autumn will not have a positive effect on any stomach. Any harvesting is best supervised by practitioners in case someone reacts to a plant material. Babies and toddlers will need much closer supervision and ideally a berry free space to avoid temptation. Specific lists can be obtained from the Royal Horticultural Society (www.rhs.org.uk).

Trees require the professional skills of a trained arboriculturalist annually to ensure that branches and the tree itself remain safe within the confines of an outdoor play area. Whilst not cheap this is essential and will also help to prolong the life, interest and qualities of the trees.

Water

Water is a concern due to the potential danger for drowning, slips and a source of potential bacteria and viruses. Practitioners can address this by explaining that all children need to learn water safety as we live on an island which has many rivers, lakes and ponds. Learning water safety will help children avoid falling in and encourage them to recognise the relevant benefits and hazards of water as well as the need to learn to swim. Any open water such as a pond within a setting should have a secure safety grid. Practitioners should ensure that any water usage is in areas that are non-slip and that children are provided with clean water for play purposes. Running water, sprinklers and sprays hold great fascination for young children and can be enormous fun on hot summer days. Giving them the power to play with water outside can be of immense value as they can develop river and lake systems as well as explore the science of hydrology. As well as supporting play, practitioners should be there to ensure there is no damage to the site or slip hazards.

Still water needs slightly different consideration to ensure that the children do not play with stagnant water. Water trays and fresh puddles are beneficial to play but containers should be given a quarterly wash out with Jeyes fluid at the appropriate concentration to avoid possible water-borne problems. Look at Claire Warden's Mindstretcher's website: www.mindstretchers.com.

Sand

Both wet and dry sand should ideally be available as they have very different properties. Outside sand is usually available on a larger scale so that the children can sit in it and explore, discover and create. Inside will require some containerisation which will need to be secure as dry sand gets everywhere including in computers, pianos, food etc. Care must be taken to ensure that the children understand its proper use. Other general rules may need to be created around throwing or transporting sand so that it does not end up in eyes and hair.

It is important to regularly dig over external sand pits to aerate them and remove leaves and rubbish. An assessment should also be undertaken annually to see if the sand needs to be replaced. Covering sand pits with suitable drainage with fishing nets drawn tightly over the surface prevents it becoming smelly and mouldy and discourages domestic pets and wildlife from fouling the sand.

Digging and mud kitchens

Mud causes mess, makes surfaces slippery and may hold a variety of bacteria, viruses and parasites. Providing the mud kitchen outside on a non-slip natural surface ensures that it is reasonably safe. Digging is valuable both for a direct purpose such as harvesting potatoes and for children's own constructional, imaginary and creative purposes. All gardening and sand toys need to be of good quality and the correct size for the children as well as being easily accessible within the sand/earth areas. Gardening tools should not be used with bare feet whereas plastic tools for sand are not ideal for proper gardening. Smaller sized garden gloves are a useful investment.

A mud kitchen with a variety of often 'second hand' utensils can be used profitably by the children in creating pies, potions and ice creams with the simple addition of earth and water. For advice look at Jan White's 'Making a Mud Kitchen' (muddyfaces.co.uk/ mud_kitchens). Contact with clean soil can be beneficial to children as it includes bacteria which we need to support healthy immune systems. However, there are also soil-borne pathogens so it is wise to use loam topsoil purchased from garden centres which is very suitable for mud play. Hand washing afterwards is essential.

Sticks and stones

Young children like sticks and stones and really engage with their arrangement. For ideas of what is possible look at the work of Andy Goldsworthy and Marc Pouyet in

Dealing with concerns

arranging natural materials. Children love to arrange them in different ways and use them for a range of imaginary possibilities. Adults however, often worry about eyes being damaged, or property. Do be aware that wood and other natural materials can easily split and crack. Whilst this also involves interesting learning it does require practitioners to be fully aware of what the children are using and how potentially hazardous they might be if misused or damaged.

Woodwork

Woodwork is like all other skill-based activities in that it needs to be taught. Once the children have learnt the necessary skills with a hammer, saw, drill etc. safely then they can start to explore wood like any other material. Generally the possibility of harm is a bruise, scrape or cut and the child learns from the experience and never does it again. The children need to be taught on a one-to-one basis so they learn the essential safety practices such as using a vice and turning fingers away from the saw, or using little taps to place a nail when hammering. Pete Moorhouse has a wonderful website which gives clear guidance for practical skills and good ideas in woodwork (www.woodworks. wordpress.com). Likewise learning to use the glue gun needs careful teaching so the children understand the great heat of the melted glue as it is extruded from the gun's tip. They also need to learn how to store the gun safely away from hands. Staff training and a policy on woodwork is advisable.

Weapon play

Young children and particularly boys will use a variety of objects to represent weapons whether practitioners want them to or not. Weapons such as guns and swords are seen as potentially harmful as they are often waved around faces and eyes. How this is handled will depend on the setting. If objects such as wooden swords are to be used then a risk assessment is sensible. If role-play is not the focus, substituting water-filled syringes and suspended balloons or empty tin cans on a wall for target practice can satisfy many schematic urges and enhance fine motor development.

Rough and tumble play and chasing games

These can be linked to weapon play but may equally result from tiggling games, running, play in a ball pool or similar. Chasing games and/or rough and tumble play may occur on a daily basis and can sometimes be misinterpreted as fighting or bullying. It is possible that an accident results from children hitting one another or stumbling over obstacles and falling because they are distracted by calling or movements from other directions. This concern is best approached as a natural physical part of child (and animal) development. Rough and tumble play allows children to let off steam, builds emotional intelligence and provides an opportunity to make mistakes and learn from them without fear of punishment.

Weather

Although children should be able to play outside in most weather conditions there are some instances when this is inadvisable such as going out in a thunderstorm or when there is black ice. Salt can be very useful for the latter but staff need to ensure that all dangerous areas are suitably treated. When there is a threat of ice, practitioners can prepare different-shaped containers with food colouring and water the night before to freeze outside overnight. These can lead to fascinating exploration the next day even if areas outside are unavailable. There is no easy rule with weather – it requires practitioner judgement as to the possible value and/or potential harm through risk assessment and follow-up by a professional decision based upon the facts.

Music and sound making

This can cause complaints from neighbours and, in some extreme cases, has led to the closure of settings. Whilst we all have a duty to respect our neighbours, the sound of children playing outside is both natural and normal. Adding triangles and temple bells may not cause a stir but a recorder blown at full force, a drum being beaten endlessly or a CD player belting out music will really annoy neighbours. Being considerate of your neighbours and checking the clock so that any noise is not endless should avoid any issues. For special events it can negate potential problems if you politely inform neighbours beforehand by letter and invite them to come and observe as valued community members.

Bicycles and wheeled toys

These are essential equipment, as some children will not have access to bikes or the space to use them at home. It is, however, important to think about how, when and where they are used. If the outdoor space is being used for obstacle courses or parachute play for example then wheeled toys/bikes are not going to be a good idea as they may lead to collisions or even fingers or toes being run over.

Fixed equipment and structures

All structures should be subject to annual safety checks for bending, warping and cracking as well as loosening around the foundations. Look for pinch and crush points, exposed mechanisms, rust, sharp points, excessive movement, be wary of missing covers as these are all symptoms of potential harm. Check all guard and handrails regularly to ensure they are secure, not loose, bent or broken. Check steps and ladders for missing or broken treads, steps or rungs. All surfaces need to be checked for cracks and loosening and impact surfaces to make sure they are not compacted, displaced or reduced in area. Drain covers should be clear and fit. Finally employ a certified supplier to check and maintain all fixed equipment, surfaces and wheeled toys etc. annually. Display your annual certificate in a central location for all to see as this reduces concern and helps parents to understand how thorough you are in attending to their child's health and safety.

Dealing with concerns

Loose parts

Stones, sticks, logs, bricks, ladders, planks, gutters, piping, tyres and tarpaulins are tools in a child's play alongside anything else they find along the way. Loose parts are important in the child starting to understand what a rich resource the environment outdoors is and the endless possibilities and connections it provides. All such resources do need a check over occasionally by practitioners and anything hazardous quietly removed.

Effective storage

Some resources such as woodwork tools or bicycles may only need to be available at certain times and can be stored away from children's reach. Everyday resources need to be at the front in labelled containers so they are accessible and can be easily put away. Boxes of equipment for fine-motor use for creative or physical skills are particularly useful if they have a handle to aid movement around the site.

Practitioners need to think about how much is available for children to use. Too many resources can end up scattered and damaged rather than carefully planned additions to a developing interest.

Conclusion

Any concern or fear from child, parent, carer or practitioner about risk, challenge and adventure must be taken seriously and addressed. We cannot assume that a child will learn positively just because they are in a wonderful place. We need to have realistic expectations for practitioners, parents and children and to 'tune in' to their concerns. This will help develop shared understandings and expectations and ensure all parties feel supported, included and valued.

CHAPTER 10

Planning adventurous activities throughout the year

Introduction

The main purpose of this chapter is to provide hands-on ideas for a range of activities which practitioners can use throughout the academic year. It begins by explaining outdoor planning in the long, medium and short terms and how this can be accomplished practically throughout the year. The chapter develops how evaluation leads onto the next planning phase by considering the range of experiences and activities which will support most young children and help to secure their interests within a meaningful environment and context. This chapter ends with some examples of activities for autumn, winter, spring and summer.

Where to start in planning activities

Practitioners should start with the children by developing warm relationships, having discussions with parents and undertaking close observation of their developmental stages, unique needs and interests as they enter the setting. This will provide guidance as to what they are interested in and their levels of development so the practitioners can consider what their next steps might be. So, for example, a child at ease in the home corner indoors could extend their learning via a mud kitchen outside. Similarly small block play indoors can be extended by a restricted set of large hollow blocks with a few planks and pieces of fabric outside for den making. For new children the core activities and opportunities will be exciting and adventurous in themselves as they will be experiencing them for the first time.

By observing children's interaction with the world around them, their schematic patterns of behaviour can also become evident and therefore schematic activities can be a good place to start. For example children with an interest in rotation will find activities such as dropping liquid paint onto a spinning Lazy Susan covered in paper and watching the effect as almost magical. Likewise swinging a funnel of paint hung from an A frame to create huge arcs of colour will fascinate them further.

The natural world also provides inspiration for learning if children are given time to discover, examine and perhaps draw or paint images of plants, leaves, fruits, seeds and vegetables. Discussing these with children can be very enlightening for the practitioner

Figure 10.1 Exploring the natural world.
Image taken from *The Power of Physical Play* © Siren Films Ltd (2014).

and assist them in finding out what children know and what they want to learn more about. Other experiences will lead to awe and wonder without any adult intervention such as dew-drops on autumn cobwebs, trying to break frozen ice in winter puddles or watching the emerging growth of daffodils as they come out in spring.

Action, improvement, development and planting plans

Within any school or setting there is most likely to be an overall improvement development plan for the premises, curriculum and other areas. The garden/outdoor area may need some careful consideration as any improvements can involve the installation of new features as well as the maintenance and repair of others. If you do not employ a gardener, the outdoor area will benefit from a yearly planting plan for the maintenance and growth of trees, bushes, flowers and vegetables.

Such plans will come from evaluation within the school/setting and of course be very individual but some typical examples are as follows:

- Developing free-flow play.
- Developing zones or areas for learning.
- Developing gender involvement.
- Developing children's gardening.
- Developing a wildlife area.
- Improving storage and access to resources.
- Improving outdoor clothing for adults and children.
- Establishing resource boxes for different weather conditions.

Such plans will need to ask the practitioners the following questions:

- What area/zone/activity/experience do you want to develop?
- Why?
- How?
- Costs?
- Who does what?
- How long?

Clearly these questions require practitioners to research possible providers, partners, costs, materials, resources and to draw up a timeline as well as find the funds, patience and perseverance to carry the plan through.

Long term curriculum planning

An effective way to start is to look at each area of the EYFS and reflect upon possible broad learning intentions alongside key activities outside. These should support and extend each aspect of each area of learning taking into account the characteristics of learning which underpin them in both prime and specific areas. For example, some children were deeply interested in the story of the Wizard of Oz. This was developed through the staff team planning lots of time for discussion about the story, leading to further language development. As discussion moved on to the characters and environments the children enjoyed a range of creative activities using different crafts and artwork making a yellow brick road and masks for the main characters. In acting out the story they used their road, emerald city and props to explore the story still further. Another group learnt some of the songs from the film and put their own dance routines together. One child realised that emerald was not only a colour but also a jewel and started the group off in exploring gemstones, which the staff set up as an interest table. Their deep engagement using magnifiers was amazing. This led to an in-depth philosophical exploration of the concept of preciousness and value. They then thought about what it means to be brave, to be heartless and so on. The focus covered the whole EYFS and engaged the children for six weeks and all the children became involved. This is clearly quite a large task to start with, but can be shared out across a staff team and them brought together by the leadership team. Once the long term plan is established, it can act as an aide memoire when planning in the medium and short term that can be used as a resource for ideas, activities and experiences. Then the long term plan only needs to be considered by staff at the start of the year to ensure any audited gaps from evaluation previously are covered or when curricular changes occur nationally.

Medium term planning

Medium term planning is the setting's term-by-term organisation of play and learning. In medium term planning an easy way to start is to look at the time of the year and focus on the activities and experiences on offer in each zone or area as relevant to the particular children, and the kinds of resources you want to provide. This will also take into account any events and special occasions so that it works strategically. For example, these resources might be tyres, crates, gutters, pipes, boxes and fabric pieces alongside specific equipment such as large construction blocks, A frames, ladders and planks so the children can create imaginative role-play environments or perhaps a scientific exploration zone for hydraulics. The children do not have access to everything all the time but with the practitioners monitoring their involvement, engagement time, whether they are playing solo, or co-operatively, within friendship groups etc., helps to then build upon, and extend their learning, through the addition or removal of particular resources or equipment.

There is often a certain degree of repetition in children's interests annually due to the seasons, festivals and weather conditions. This means that the seasonal change alone can provide a very rich source of children's interest. These repeatable experiences can be planned for by setting up resource boxes of certain books, role-play clothes and equipment so they can be provided as and when the children need them and in manageable quantities.

Other basic resources can be great starting points such as brooms and buckets to sweep up leaves in the autumn, explorer jackets with notebooks, cameras and field guides when on mini-beast hunts or tools, hard hats, decorating brushes and ladders when the interest is on building.

Short term planning

Short term planning is often called fortnightly or weekly planning as it is generally reviewed fortnightly, weekly and daily as staff witness children's interests, dispositions, requests, needs and frustrations emerging and adapt accordingly. Practitioners should avoid becoming over-enthusiastic in provision, resulting in over resourcing and temporary chaos. The phrase 'less is more' is useful as it allows practitioners to carefully phase in via their short term planning, the inclusion of resources which add to, challenge and extend learning potential and possibilities for the children.

Daily planning cannot respond to each and every child's interests and needs but it can adapt to particular requests from the children or the perceived needs of particular groups who need more specialised activities. Written plans should never stop practitioners responding intuitively or following the children's lead. There should always be scenarios that allow planning rules to be broken so opportunities aren't missed such as:

- a robin flies into the classroom;
- it starts snowing;
- 'I forgot to get...';
- 'XXX was sick, so we...'.

Unpredictable events can often be maximised as learning experiences rather than sticking rigidly to timetables, protocols and procedures and often result in the children being happier and learning more. It won't always be easy and children won't always respond as one would desire. They may be tired, unwell or just grumpy and when asked to tidy up, to leave a snail alone, to not pick flowers or just to listen may not show the environment the respect the practitioner thinks they should.

Evaluation

Evaluation is about the careful reflection by the staff team of the circumstances, achievements and areas for development in the relevant period. Evaluation should be carried out in the short term at the end of each day, week or fortnight as well as at the end of term or quarter. An annual evaluation is also good practice as this feeds into the annual improvement, development or action plan.

For short term evaluation it is often best to use sticky notes or labels on the back of the planning sheet to record what has gone well and why, and what needs to be adapted. These can then be used at the evaluation meeting for the week or fortnight to guide planning for the next period of time. Such evaluations can also lead to the identification of focus children; groups of children; areas or zones of learning for future observation as well as clear planning for forthcoming events, festivities and transitions. This then leads back into future medium and long term planning so that any evident gaps are planned for in future activities and experiences.

Planning for heuristic/natural play

Heuristic play is closely linked to outdoor play in that many of the natural materials are found and collected outside but used elsewhere inside the nursery. This two-way process mirrors the two main environmental areas. So the feathers and skeleton leaves find their way to the light box and the bigger pebbles and dried cones to some of the treasure baskets with the toddlers. Goldschmied and Jackson (2004) initiated these innovative baskets so that the individual child has the chance to learn and discover for themselves without adult interference. The provocative baskets are designed to stimulate curiosity and give an opportunity to create a bridge between outdoors and indoors on really inclement days or for children whose access is not always so easy. With babies under the age of 2 the selection of the items in the treasure needs careful risk assessment as they can easily find their way up noses and into ears as well as being eaten. An unbreakable mirror made for such young babies can also be a source of exploration. However, for the twos and threes, bigger items are explored much more safely. The increasing mobility also means they can more easily access the outdoors themselves.

Basic provision/resource planning for the seasons

The crucial thing about the seasons is being ready for different weather conditions so the waterproof, wind proof and cold-resistant clothing is available in the colder, wetter months and sun screen and hats in the hotter ones.

If you are limited by staffing ratios think of easy ways to ensure the children who should be outside are outside if you cannot provide free-flow for all. Armbands or hair scrunchies are excellent ways to easily identify who should be where. This can be achieved by a rota, which prioritises the children who need the experience most whilst providing equity for all.

Prepare laminated lists of outdoor activities for staff to use outside to respond to and provoke children's interests with added stories, rhymes, poems and songs. Laminated photographs of weather and nature can be used as further ways of extending interests. A set of simple reference books or laminated identification cards for mini-beasts, birds and pond life can also be useful.

Toys and equipment outdoors throughout the year

Traditional outdoor toys such as bikes and scooters are very popular with children and especially to those who have less or no access to them at home. Some other toys require different or refined skills such as the space hopper, frisbee, bats and balls which may inhibit their use by some children.

Old favourites such as hopscotch, basketball, parachute and skittles, quoits etc. may prove popular too. The beanbag in the bucket is popular with a tally chart nearby to keep the score and build mathematical learning and you can add numerals or letters to add further learning potential. Different equipment can be very useful at different times of the year such as the parachute when there are many new children as a means of including them or just after heavy rain. Equally bicycles and wheeled toys are quickly assembled after a storm which has prevented other resourcing of activities. In very hot weather buckets of water and decorating brushes, a paddling pool to dip feet into or the sprinkler are valid experiences as well as ways to keep children cool.

Autumn activities

Autumn often gives that glorious combination of lovely sunny days with cool or chilly nights. For many young children it is often when they start nursery. The changes in the season bring the chance to gather in the harvest, sweep up leaves, dig over flower and vegetable beds, plant bulbs and revel in the changing colours of autumn leaves. These can all act as points of interest and stimulus for further learning. Leaf printing is an age-old favourite but one which provides for learning across the EYFS.

Match the leaf

This needs to be created in advance with laminated leaves of different types or pairs. The children then have to hunt for their own. This can lead to counting how many different types of leaves were collected as well as comparing their different features.

Creative murals

These can be made with natural items on the floor as a picture or carpet by collecting conkers, acorns and leaves to arrange alongside stones, feathers etc. creatively. Fabric and hessian also add a range of dimensions to such murals and photography allows the murals to be kept and displayed effectively. Pressing natural materials into thin clay and then cutting them out can create very special mobiles once given a hanging hole and dried.

Cobweb/skeleton leaf collection

You can make webs by using PVA glue squeezed web-like on to a large plastic sack and then sprinkled with glitter and other shiny objects. This is left to dry and then peeled off and hung in trees and bushes for decorative purposes.

Find the King or Queen conker/acorn/cone

This is a challenge to find the largest, shiniest conker or acorn. This can be applied to any natural object, e.g. cabbage, carrot.

Sycamore or ash helicopters

These are simply collected and then launched into the air to flutter and spin down.

Making monster and fairy homes from wood, moss, leaves etc.

Again, photography can be used to capture the moment alongside the scripted description of the child's explanation. A glue gun can also be useful in securing pieces together strongly if you wish to keep them.

King/Queen of the forest

This is a chance for children to try out a role and create a crown from flexible twigs and natural materials. They can be particularly charming if based upon a willow circle woven with flowers, feathers and leaves.

Hiding in and throwing leaves

Self explanatory and great fun!

Painting with berries and vegetables

This is easily achieved by collecting berries to squash for paint (e.g. elderberries and blackberries for purple, crab apples for yellow, sloes for blue, and grass for green) with a pestle and mortar with water. Push through a sieve or tea strainer. Also try vegetables such as onion, carrots and beetroot. Ask the children for suggestions too.

Lavender or herb play dough

This requires a plain play dough to which the children can add herbs using scissors to shred small pieces which they then press into the dough to both create aromatic and textural experiences.

Knuckle bones or fives

Acorns or small pebbles are balanced on the back of the hand, thrown up into the air and caught. For smaller hands adapt the number of items.

Fog and frost box

Collect different trays and transparent containers to fill with water and leave outside over night to discover what happens. (Hats, scarves and gloves for those children who have forgotten them are useful.) You can use sea salt and other household substances to investigate what will melt the ice.

Winter activities

Winter can restrict learning outside if it is severely cold. However, every day brings new possibilities especially with weather changes. Cold weather means that suitable clothing and physical activity is essential so that children stay warm. Wind often excites children but care should be taken if they are close to large trees. The provision of resources will be less varied than in warmer weather but the environment itself provides huge interest for children. Ice, frost and snow provide the basis of science and technological exploration through simple observation to greater challenges such as 'Save the Snowman from Melting'!

Enjoying snow and ice without additions

Children are joyous on icy and snowy mornings! Although the adults may have had a really challenging time the sheer awe and wonder of seeing a frosty or snowy coating over everything is absolutely not to be missed.

Ice games

Skittles, hoops and balls can create an understanding of the qualities of frozen water and how fast things travel across it.

Building or sculpting

The children could make an igloo, ice castle, ice animal, ice inuksuk, snow monsters, dens or snow people. They can also make snow angels by lying down on the snow and waving your arms up and down.

Save the snowman

This can keep children occupied problem solving with only a few handfuls of snow to make a very small snowman and then trying various ways to both melt and preserve him with items such as a water bottle, foil, foam rubber, bubble wrap, a scarf, etc.

Make your own icicles and ice mobiles

Freeze leaves and natural objects over night in small containers with string between to hang in the trees and bushes.

Windy day box

This should contain resources to make items such as wind flags, spinners, nylon scarves, windmills, kites and ribbon sticks with fabric, short canes or paper, curtain rings, streamers, bubbles, windsocks, balloons, confetti, wind chimes, foam frisbees, pom-poms, fabric balls and a parachute.

A-frame creative music

This can be made using climbing frame equipment and a strong rod with pots and pans strung from it with wooden spoons and beaters to make music. Be aware that endless sound may annoy neighbours so be careful when and where you site such activities.

Natural decorations

Use sticks and cones to make wreaths, stars, spirals, animals, angels and candle decorations using flowers pots, jars etc. as candle holders.

Bird food holders

These can be made with Tetra pack milk and juice packs with a string or cones coated in fat and seeds. Be aware of food allergies though.

Treasure boxes

These work well if you freeze small items such as plastic jewels or even chocolate gold coins in ice cream containers filled with water. The effort to extract them is a real challenge for some children and then all can follow up with lots of counting and comparisons.

Snow and ice box

This can provide different stimuli if the contents include a variety of containers to freeze, a hot water bottle, bubble wrap, winter clothing, a small tarpaulin to sit on, camera, and food colouring to drop on the snow. As a special treat chocolate foil-covered coins give great impetus to break apart the ice and get inside!

Spring activities

The early signs of spring can be brought indoors to allow close observation of the growth of bulbs, the emergence of catkins and pussy willow. The weather can be very varied and need the creativity of staff to adapt to all seasons over a few days. This means resourcing can be challenging. Quickly moveable activities such as chalk mark making, kite flying, parachute play and ball games are very useful.

Mark making box

This could include a selection of clipboards, pens, pencils chalks, crayons, white and blackboards, decorator's brushes and rollers, plant sprayers, notebooks and a variety of paper, alphabet sticks, wooden letter and stones. Finger painting on plastic sheets or the outside of low windows is easy and you can take prints off by pressing paper on top so you can keep a copy of the images and patterns created. Other resources linked to role-play such as the garage or the garden centre will lead to wider learning opportunities. Writing caddies/clipboards and writer's bum bags if usefully stocked will also inspire writing when linked to role-play etc.

Soil factories

These can create an opportunity for children to dig up earth and then use a variety of sieves both created and purpose made to create fine tilth for seed sowing and miniature gardens.

Container planting

Using old wellington boots, sieves, pots and pans as containers can really excite children's interest in gardening and add real reasons for talk. I have also seen guttering fixed to a wall at different heights to grow lettuce etc. very effectively in a small space. Michael the Education Officer at the Chelsea Physic Garden has a wonderful collection of plants growing in containers for the food stuff that comes from them including oats growing in a porridge box lined with plastic and a small olive tree in an olive oil can from a restaurant.

Balancing beams and wobble boards

These can be both purpose made and home crafted pieces of equipment. They can really benefit children's problem solving skills if they collaborate on making their own.

Twig sculptures

These can be made using string, wool or twine with a variety of different widths and sizes of twigs. Feathers, leaves etc. can be added for decorative purposes.

Rainy Day Box

This should include a collection of umbrellas, tarpaulins, wellies, waterproof fabrics and different shaped containers to collect rain in. Food colouring, cooking oil and washing up liquid can be added to puddles for science. Small plastic and foil containers with pipettes, syringes and small scoops with bubble mixture and home-made wands of different shapes are also huge fun.

Pond dipping

This is a very good way of developing patience and observation skills. Small aquarium nets, white trays and dishes are the equipment required along with a simple identification guide.

Bug hunt or shake the bush on a white cloth

This is a smaller form of a mini-beast hunt particularly suited for smaller outside areas. By placing a light coloured cloth under the bush it is easier to see and identify the creatures which emerge. A simple identification guide and magnifiers are also required.

Making nests

Making nests using twigs, straw, moss, and feathers etc. challenges children's abilities to weave and twine natural materials together. The problem solving aspects of creating a safe nest which the real eggs don't fall out of add another level of challenge. Use plastic eggs if your prefer or if you have a child with food allergies.

Easter Egg hunts

Wooden or plastic eggs can be substitutes for chocolate ones but work equally well.

Mud pies, cakes, sculptures and mud drawing and casts

These are all easily created with some fairly liquid mud. Casts and sculptures require slightly less fluid mud if the drawings are to be cast into Plaster of Paris and set. Draw on scrap or newspaper if you don't want to use pristine paper. Collect old pots and pans and buy plastic and metal sieves, funnels, spoons etc. from Pound shops.

Summer activities

In summer you need to consider different clothing and equipment with suitable hats which cover the neck and ears, high factor sun cream, insect repellent and plenty of water to drink. British summers can be very hot for periods of time as well as cool and wet so waterproof gear is also essential. As weather may vary a blend of activities is likely. The vegetation should really develop and provide children with opportunities to learn how to weed, thin out, water vegetables as well as harvesting strawberries and early potatoes which can be grown in tubs and pots. Observation of mini-beasts and water and sand play on fine days are essential parts of childhood. Food for picnics and expeditions should be packed in cool bags so it will stay cool and safe to eat in the heat.

Making petal perfume

Fallen petals from scented flowers such as roses are collected and soaked in water. The resulting 'perfume' can be poured into plastic bottles.

Grass heads

Cut off the feet of tights or stocking and fill them with sawdust mixed with grass seed. The seed needs to be placed near the top to create the "hair" and then a face can be added with felt tip markers.

Picnic or pavement cafe role-plays

These can serve home-made elderflower cordial, fruit/vegetables from the garden or home-made sandwiches etc. Have a collection of table cloths, cutlery, plastic crockery and glasses, pencils and small notepads, laminated menus, play money, aprons, trays etc.

Pattern painting

This is achieved by providing paint in shallow trays and then a collection of items to press into the paint and then put onto a large sheet of paper to create patterns. Natural items such as leaves and feathers are very effective alongside wellington boots, junk materials, fabric and things such as orange rind.

Bear hunt box

This will add real role-play to just creeping through long grass with trays of gravel, sand, compost etc. The possibilities are endless if you add music, resources to make a cave and a bear costume etc.

Tiny town role-play

Use a small garden tray to create a tiny town or garden for mini role-play in a tin or tray. Recording it on the flip camera and showing it later on the whiteboard can also lead to much discussion.

Colour sticky cards

These are purpose bought cards created using double sided sticky sheets. One side is stuck to thick card and then the protective paper is removed so each child can have a square to collect and stick on fallen flower petals, small leaves, feathers etc.

Old pots and pans orchestra

Create these from any old kitchen utensils hung on a strong line with spoons etc. to 'play' with.

Recycled coloured bottles

Bottles of different shapes and sizes can be filled with a variety of different coloured water plus items such as glitter and buttons. Seal with strong plastic tape and using string can be hung up as decoration to catch the light or just leave on a low wall for the children to explore and discuss.

Dam and bridge building

This can be created by bring water via a hose or watering cans and to a sandpit or similar. Then if you add natural resources such as leaves, foil and plastic containers, corks and paper the children will invent leaf boats with mast and leaf sails.

Water play

This requires guttering, pipes and a variety of containers and pourers linked to shallow water trays. Use 'elephant tape' to fix the various parts together with items such as funnels and thinner tubes. Crates and fruit boxes, old plastic pots and spare hosepipes are also useful. If you can create enough flow of water say down a slope as we do into the amphitheatre, you can play 'Pooh sticks' and boats using straws and leaves. A large bucket and decorating brushes also go a long way to developing mark making and co-ordination skills too. A large water container with a tap to take water to where it is needed

Adventurous activities throughout the year

for role-play etc. can also be a really useful stimulus and will allow the children to control the flow of water themselves.

Weaving on railings/fences, making dream catchers or your own loom

Use string or wool as the basic warp/weft created by the adults and then give the children an array of natural and artificial items to weave into the tapestry. Anything from leaves, feathers, and ribbon and plastic carrier bags can be used to decorate. Flexible willow or plastic can be used to create dream catcher frames too.

Wimbledon role-play

Use air flow balls hung from a strong line or similar that the children can hit with plastic rackets.

Number and other hunts

These need to be pre-prepared and scattered around the garden. Numerals, letters, shapes both 2D and 3D, patterns, dinosaurs, book characters are all huge motivators for children to work together to find all of the collection.

Group shapes

This requires a lot of co-operation and collaboration between the children who, whilst a drum beats, form the required shape, e.g. square.

Sundials

These can easily be made with a stick in the ground and a cardboard circular collar placed around it to record the shadow lines on.

Stone skimming

This requires a pond or large puddle and is an activity for increasing dexterity but also great for trajectory schema.

Sleeping lions

The good old party game played outside. Excellent for calming children down!

Daisy and other flower chains

This requires a daisy covered lawn and some manual dexterity! A thick piece of sisal rope can also be good to decorate with leaves and flowers.

Dribbling sand castles

Use fine, wet sand which is very fluid and dribble it down through your hands to make thin, pointed castles.

Stone/pebble pictures, sculptures and castles, shell and beach mosaics

Driftwood and a glue gun with fishing line can create some unusual sculptures and mosaics.

Corn dollies

These can be made with paper drinking straws if you cannot obtain real straw. Whilst children can learn to fold and cut the straws they can be very creative in making a variety of dolls, figures and scarecrows to decorate the garden.

Garden centre role-play

Provide a selection of gardening tools, gloves, pots and boxes, watering cans, labels and pencils, catalogues and seeds, gardening magazines and compost.

Sunshine box

This could consist of solar paper, X-rays, thermometer, sunshade, hats, bubble making equipment etc.

Year-round experiences and activities

A range of adaptable, flexible activities can be provided all year round. This does not mean that the equipment should be available all the time but rather used appropriately to develop children's interests and needs at the ideal time. Some will be weather dependent whilst others can be used on any day. Variety is important but should be set alongside the opportunity for children to explore resources in depth in order to develop their confidence and skills.

Tree climbing

Some children love the chance to see the world from a different angle or perspective. Try to find a special climbing tree or a fallen tree.

Dens

A great source of enthusiastic collaborative play. Den making is fun and is built upon the schematic desire to make a shelter and that innate nesting instinct. Temporary den structures made with clothes horses or purpose built frames provide very different enclosures to the one we have which is a very permanent Kent barn type structure which is tall enough for adults to stand up in. Over the years we have also created several willow dens with a willow artist. The children are adept at creating dens with a vast array of materials from large cardboard boxes to the A frames, canes and plastic pipes with large fabric pieces, netting, rope or even small tarpaulins. A camouflage net is also a great investment alongside a range of gripper pegs and tape to hold them together.

Cardboard boxes

A supply of very large cardboard boxes creates very active collaborative and creative play. Boxes are different to toys as they are open-ended and provide the freedom to do as you wish in a way. They can be made into homes, dens, tunnels etc. Even when the structures that had been created have been destroyed the children continue to play with them using the broken and flattened pieces as walls, bird wings and as a starting point for other games. When I asked the children why they seem to love the boxes so much I was told it was 'Because we can play with them again and again in lots of ways.' Interestingly this seems to be regardless of gender, age or ability.

Exploring/wonder boxes and mini-beast hunts

These are again popular at different times of the year but particularly on sunnier days. However, even on the coldest day a log, branch or stone can be lifted to reveal woodlice, centipedes and worms. The children may or may not want to handle the mini-beasts but they should be encouraged to return everything back exactly to how they found it. Ensure you have notebooks, pens, cameras, magnifiers, binoculars, maps, torches, and high visibility vests with pockets for all the gear. Collect items such as fossils, shells, gemstones, old household artefacts for the children to explore, discuss and wonder about. Their questions will astound you! Match boxes make great wonder boxes on a different scale.

'Mirror-to-the-sky'

This is a metaphysical experience which involves a small group gathering round a large (unbreakable mirror) to look at the sky or trees. Smaller hand-held mirrors can also work very effectively too and encourage rich language without stiff necks.

Tree hugging

This can be fun with blindfolds or with a really large tree by linking hands together to surround it. The experience encourages children to explore with their fingertips to feel how different trees have different bark textures and fissures depending upon the type, shape and size of tree. The blindfolds help to concentrate their senses on the challenge.

Sensory bags and feely boxes

These can encourage the sense of touch and smell by the placement of different natural materials within semi-sealed cardboard boxes or fabric bags such as crushed herbs, garlic, pine cones etc.

Sticks, shells and stones

Build up collections of pebbles, fossils, rocks, gems, short sturdy sticks and slices of timber etc. These can be used with small role-play people, animals and vehicles as well as to create decorative arrangements with feathers, fabric etc. in a builder's tray or on the ground. A collection of books such as *Stick Man* by Julia Donaldson and Axel Scheffler and *Stanley's Stick* by John Hegley and Neal Layton will be popular too.

Mystery walks and bear hunts

These can be set up with trays of different materials such as sand, mud, gravel, pebbles and a rope to guide the children across, perhaps with bare feet and blindfolds after some previous experience with footwear on.

Scavenging and exploring

These are ways to involve and interest most children. The main aim to collect items within the garden, park etc. which are loose and not growing, e.g. dead leaves, feathers, stones, sticks, nuts, seeds, pebbles, snail shells and so on. Egg boxes, stick cards and a variety of bags and containers can be used to collect and display the found treasures which can then be used to create sculptures, mobiles etc.

Night time activities

Special night time events are also huge fun and often a very different learning experience for young children who rarely go out in the dark for long. Your garden or outside area can be used to celebrate the festivals that surround Christmas including Diwali and Hanukkah by singing festive songs around a tree or similar in the garden decorated by the children. Families can come back to nursery and enjoy hot chocolate and home-made cakes.

Rainforest or other themed story telling boxes

These are a good way to start adventures off. Put in a camouflage net, helmets, walkie-talkies, binoculars, telescopes, notebooks and pencils, maps, wild animal books, compass, torch, water bottles, pop-up tent, back packs etc.

Adventurous activities throughout the year

Chalk and black boards

These can easily be created with blackboard paint on flat surfaces. We also use our plastic screens for painting with powder paints as they easily wash down afterwards.

Art/science challenges

Having worked with our resident scientist Dr Jasmine over numerous occasions we have seen how close the boundaries of art and science are. Two of our favourite activities include photo box paint poppers and pendulum painting. The latter uses an A frame to suspend a funnel on a length of string which is topped up with different colours of liquid paint and then spun over paper or fabric sheets can create some fantastic rotational and arc images which schematically and scientifically are interesting. Photo box paint poppers use 35mm film boxes (or similar with tight lids) half an Alka Seltzer tablet and a teaspoon of powder paint. Add a little vinegar, place the pot lid down on a large sheet of paper and stand well back!

Garage/car wash/window cleaning/painting role-play

You can use the large hollow blocks to create a ramp to rise up the vehicles for washing. A few tyres, watering cans, the hose and buckets with cloths, brushes, rollers and sponges add to the reality. Another box of car parts and some tools such as spanners alongside car manuals and magazines can easily develop into garage role-play.

Road safety/builders' yard role-play

This includes resources such as hard hats, cones, signs, spades, wheel barrows, plans, and wheeled vehicles. Plastic writable clipboards and signs can add a real opportunity for mark making too.

Logs and shrubbery areas

These can be used creatively by young children to make their own hiding places as well as a means to create dens. Logs make great stepping stones too.

Milk and mushroom crates

These can be used to build structures, obstacle courses, vehicles or for creative activities such as weaving. Items such as cable drums found in skips can also be added for natural tables and display areas.

Single or special loose items to collect

There are a few key resources, which can be used across the year in a variety of flexible and creative ways. They are not typically available but are the 'loose parts', which add value and possibility to young children's learning. The following are resources I would highly recommend acquiring for an early years school or setting:

- a length of the very thickest rope you can find plus other lengths and sizes of rope;
- a builder's tray or two;
- a big block of wood for hammering;
- a bow saw for co-operative tasks;
- loppers for den making to cut wood lengths to the required size;
- spring pegs, jumbo gripper pegs and giant pegs for fastening fabrics to dens etc.;
- silver fabric tape and masking tape;
- photo pockets to display recent activities and experiences;
- sari and other fabrics;
- camouflage netting;
- a good ground sheet and tarpaulins of different sizes;
- artefacts and items for wonder boxes on different scales.

Summary

Each season and weather type has its joys and challenges. Adventures can happen at any time. What is required is careful observation, quality planning and in-depth evaluation to maximise adventurous possibilities and extensions whatever the venue or weather.

Outdoor play policy

Chelsea Open Air Nursery School and Children's Centre

Outdoor Play

The policy above will be monitored and evaluated following the policy cycle at

Chelsea Open Air

Date of establishment: 1997
Date of Last Review: 2013
Date of next Review: 2016

Approved by Governors on:

Signed on behalf of Chelsea Open Air Nursery School and Children's Centre:

_____

Signed on behalf of the Governing Body:

_____

OUTDOOR PLAY POLICY

Introduction

Why have an outdoor play policy?

Play is an essential part of every child's life and vital to the processes of human development. It provides the mechanism for children to explore the world around them and the medium through which skills are developed and practised. It is essential for physical, emotional and spiritual growth, intellectual and educational development and acquiring social and behavioural skills.

N.V.C.C.P. Charter

COA Ethos

We believe that children learn through outdoor play, which complements and enhances their indoor learning.

We aim to:

- Promote good quality, challenging, safe and accessible play for all children.
- Provide well-planned engaging activities outside similar but different to indoors.
- Provide an environment to extend and improve children's learning and wellbeing regardless of the weather.
- Make the most of an environment over which we have little control.
- Expand children's horizons of what learning can be experienced outside.
- Fulfil the requirements of the Early Years Foundation Stage outdoors as well as indoors.

Learning, Teaching and Caring Opportunities

1. Be independent.
2. Be inventive and creative.
3. Make their own choices and decisions.
4. Take risks and solve problems.
5. Learn and play in diverse groupings, which are not always controlled or supported by an adult.
6. Develop individual interests and find own boundaries.
7. Communicate, co-operate and negotiate with others.
8. Experience a sense of adventure, excitement and fun.
9. Develop fine and gross-motor skills.
10. Develop physical skills for supporting emotional wellbeing.
11. Develop an appreciation of things seen, touched, smelt and heard.
12. Develop a sense of awe and wonder in the natural world.
13. Experience the seasons in all their richness.
14. Develop knowledge and understanding of the natural environment, for examples life cycles.

15 Develop and extend cognitive skills (maths, science, geography, language, reasoning, logic) through active experience, discovery and practice.

16 Engage in new experiences.

17 Revisit, repeat, re-live, recall, build-on and adapt previous experiences.

18 Opportunities to experiment, observe, hypothesise, draw conclusions.

19 Experience quiet and secluded areas, for example, dens, tents.

... But as well as all this, there is something more ... something *very, very* special, which we delight in and value enormously about our garden. Something which we believe to be part of the very essence of childhood. This is the world of imagination, fairy-tale, magic, pretend, enchantment, story ... that whole exciting world of fantasy.

Policy into Practice

1 There must be two members of staff (not including staff who support children with individual needs) at all times, unless there are very few children outside (five or fewer).

2 To teach the children care and respect for each other, plants, animals, wildlife and the environment.

3 Children may move large or heavy objects, planks, boxes, or ladders when appropriate round the garden to make their own constructions. We show the children the best way to move these objects independently, or with a friend and encourage the children to ask us to help test their construction for safety.

4 The children may sit or kneel next to the pond but not walk on the protective grid or throw things into the water.

5 Children may use woodwork tools following our guidelines for woodwork, and gardening tools with adult supervision.

6 Sand should stay in the sand pit, unless being specifically used elsewhere.

7 Children are encouraged to wear wellington boots when the garden is wet and muddy.

8 Any climbing construction put up by ourselves for the children must be tested for safety before the children use it.

9 To teach children safety rules when climbing. Never to climb with toys in their hands. Never to push, pull or hold onto their friends when climbing. Not to play in role-play shoes, long flowing dressing up clothes or coats like cloaks for safety reasons.

10 To provide children with the broad and balanced curriculum indoors and out.

11 To designate areas for specific equipment for example, wheeled toys, space hoppers and stilts.

12 Wheelchairs to access all areas of the garden where possible.

13 The wooden edge of the amphitheatre or the perspex is not a climbing area.

14 To provide children with honestly appropriate answers to their questions about the world around them.

15 Children can go barefoot when the weather is warmer. Socks and shoes will be stored safely.

16 Small fires are supervised by a staff member constantly and have been properly risk assessed.

17 Make full use of prevailing weather conditions after risk assessing the circumstances.

Observation template

Name:
Context:
Observation:
Significance and possible next steps:
Observed by: Date:

Planning template: Adult-focused activity

Name of adult:

Area of curriculum:
What I want the children to learn:
Resources:
Activity:
Vocabulary:
Evaluation:

Daily workshop plan

WB:	Tactile	Creative	Imaginative Play	Music	Construction	Maths	CLL	K&U	ICT	Physical	Garden	Special Events
Monday												
Tuesday												
Wednesday												
Thursday												
Friday												

Red Pen = Garden   Black Pen = Inside   Highlighted = Focus Activity

Weekly planning template

Learning intention/ knowledge/skills/attitude	Areas & resources inside & out for spontaneous learning	Planned activities & experiences	Adult input & specific language input
Personal, Social & Emotional			
Communication, Language & Literacy			
Mathematical Development			
Knowledge & Understanding of the World			
ICT			
Physical Development			
Creative Development			

Red = Garden   Green = Specific SEN   Black = Inside   Highlighted = Focus Activities

Guidelines for helpers offsite

Chelsea Open Air Nursery School and Children's Centre
Guidelines for Helpers
(Offsite Activities)

The policy above will be monitored and evaluated following the policy cycle at Chelsea Open Air

Date of establishment:
Date of last Review:
Date of next Review:
Approved by Governors on:

Signed on behalf of Chelsea Open Air Nursery School and Children's Centre:

_____

Signed on behalf of the Governing Body:

_____

Information for Helpers on Offsite Activities

1   You have been asked to support and extend the children's learning by accompanying them on a visit/expedition. This will involve you in talking to them pointing out matters of interest and encouraging their interest and questions.

2   You will be asked to hold the hands of two children maximum. Sadly, this means that you cannot push a buggy or hold the hand of a toddler.

3   Be aware of the children's safety at all times, and if in doubt check any concerns with the member of staff in charge. If anything serious happens carefully follow the instructions given by the member of staff if at all possible, if not use common sense and remove yourself and the children to a place of safety as soon as possible.

4   Do ask the member of staff in charge for any detailed information you require about the visit/activity before you leave the school, as it is difficult to pay close attention to both the children in your charge and adult conversation at the same time.

5   Clearly, no helping adult should be smoking, drinking alcohol, using a mobile phone or behaving inappropriately when giving care and attention to small children.

6   A small rucksack or similar is a useful item to carry your essentials and enables you to have free hands.

7   The bottom line is – treat your charges as you would like your own children to be treated. If you have any worries or difficulties, consult the member of staff in charge immediately.

Weather boxes

Activities for Rainy Days

RESOURCES	ACTIVITIES
Rainy day clothing ● Coats ● Wellington boots ● All-in-one suits ● Umbrellas	Collect rain water in different containers and measure how much has fallen. Use containers made from different materials including paper/card. Which container collected the most rain water? Why? What happened to the cardboard container when it was in the rain? (PSRN and KUW)
Different-sized containers ● Bottles ● Cups ● Trays ● Bowls ● Plates ● Jars ● Tubes Include containers made out of different materials (e.g. glass, plastic, paper, card and foil)	**Shrinking puddles** Investigate puddles by drawing round them with chalks and watching to see how quickly the water evaporates and the puddle shrinks. Discuss what has happened with the children. Where has the water gone? (KUW) **Splashing** When the children are dressed in all-in-one suits they will love jumping and walking through the puddles. Who can make the biggest splash? How deep is the puddle? (PSED and KUW)
Different materials ● Fabric/cloth ● Wood ● Paper ● Plastic ● Foil ● Glass	**Waterproof coat for Teddy** Show the children a selection of different materials and encourage them to predict which will make the best waterproof coat for Teddy. Investigate, test and make a coat for Teddy. Which materials made the best waterproof coat? (KUW)
Mark-making implements ● Paint brushes ● Chalks Tarpaulins to create dens and shelter. Sand - what happens when it gets wet? (i.e. consistency, texture etc.).	**Spider webs** Look for spider webs to observe how the rain droplets catch on the different threads and talk about the shapes and patterns they can see. (KUW and PSRN) **Listening to the rain** Listen to the sound the rain makes as it falls into containers made from different materials. Encourage the children to talk about the differences between the sounds. What does the rain sound like when it lands in the foil container/glass container? (KUW and CLL)

Appendix 7

Food colouring
Ready mixed paint
Cooking oil
Powder paint
Paper plates

Rain makers
- Empty soda pop bottles with lids
- Beans
- Seeds
- Pasta
- Rice

Rippling water

Observe what happens to the puddles or containers of water when rain droplets land on them or a pebble is thrown into them (i.e. ripples, splash). What happens if you blow the water? (KUW)

Mark-making

Collect rain water in containers and use the paint brushes to make marks on walls, ground etc. Use the chalks to make marks on the wet ground. (CLL)

Rainbow puddles

Add drops of food colouring or ready mixed paint to puddles and observe what happens. What happens if you add a small amount of cooking oil? e.g. creates a rainbow effect. (CD)

Rain Painting

Put drops of food colouring or powder paint onto a paper plate and hold the plate in the rain for about a minute. Watch as the drops of rain mix with the paint to create patterns. Encourage the children to look at the designs created and talk about them. (CD)

Rain music

Encourage the children to make rain makers using empty soda pop bottles. Fill bottles with dry sand, beans, seeds, pasta or rice and screw the lids on tight. Shake or slowly tip the bottles upside down to create the rain sound and sing songs. (CD)

BOOKS

The Rainy Day, Anna Milbourne
Alfie's Weather, Shirley Hughes
Elmer's Weather, David McKee
Postman Pat's Rainy Day, John Cunliffe
Ruby's Rainy Day, Rosemary Wells

Kipper's Rainy Day, Mick Inkpen
Kipper's Book of Weather, Mick Inkpen
Maisie's Wonderful Weather Book, Lucy Cousins
Spot's Rainy Day, Eric Hill
Rainy Days, Jennifer S Burke

SONGS AND RHYMES

Little Raindrops

This is the sun, high up in the sky.
A dark cloud suddenly comes sailing by.
These are the raindrops,
Pitter, pattering down.
Watering the flower seeds
That grow under the ground.

Fun in the Rain

(to the tune of 'Three Blind Mice')

Rain, rain, rain. Rain, rain, rain.
Dribble, dribble, splosh!
Dribble, dribble, splosh!
Grab your boots, your coat, and hat,
Jump in a puddle and go KERSPLAT!
Stomp about and become a drowned rat,
Rain, rain, rain. Rain, rain, rain.

It's Raining, It's Pouring

It's raining, it's pouring,
The old man is snoring.
He bumped his head, and he went to bed,
And he couldn't get up in the morning.

Incy Wincy Spider

Incy wincy spider,
Climbed up the water spout.
Down came the rain and washed the spider out.
Out came the sunshine and dried up all the rain.
So Incy wincy spider climbed up the spout again.

I Hear Thunder

(to the tune of 'Frere Jacques')

I hear thunder, I hear thunder,
Hark, don't you?
Hark, don't you?
Pitter patter raindrops,
Pitter patter raindrops,
I'm wet through.
So are you.

Doctor Foster

Doctor Foster went to Gloucester,
In a shower of rain.
He stepped in a puddle,
right up to his middle.
And never went there again.

Activities for Windy Days

RESOURCES	ACTIVITIES
Windy day clothing ● Coats ● All-in-one suits **Items that catch the wind** ● Ribbons ● Scarves ● Streamers ● Flags ● Kites ● Confetti ● Parachute ● Wind socks ● Bubbles ● Windmills **Make your own kite/flag** ● Sticks ● Straws ● Paper ● Card ● Newspaper ● Tissue ● Plastic acetate ● Scissors ● Tape or sellotape ● String or wool Wind chimes (wood & metal) **Make your own wind chimes** ● Coat hangers ● String or wool ● Spoons (metal & plastic) ● Bells ● Lollypop sticks ● Egg cups (wood & plastic) **Paper aeroplanes** ● Ordinary paper ● Newspaper ● Tissue paper ● Foil paper ● Greaseproof paper ● Sugar paper Ready mixed paint ● Paper plates or sheets of paper Washing line and pegs Washing up bowl Selection of dolls clothes	**Watch the wind** Let the children play with ribbons, scarves, streamers and sheets and encourage them to run with them behind them to catch the wind. Attach windsocks to tree branches or fences and watch how they move in the wind. Throw confetti or leaves into the air and watch how they float and catch the wind. Blow bubbles and watch as they float and drift away. Hold a windmill and watch as it spins around. Encourage the children to talk about what they have observed and what happened. (KUW) **Fly a kite** Use different-shaped kites and show the children how to fly them and hold them correctly. Watch the movements they make as they fly in the sky. (PSRN and PD) **Make a kite** Investigate, make and test which materials would make a good kite. Which kite flew the highest? Which kite stayed in the air the longest? (KUW and CD) **Wind chimes** Hang a variety of different wind chimes outside made out of wood and metal and listen to the sounds they make as they catch the wind. Make your own wind chimes using different materials (e.g. metal and plastic spoons, bells, lollypop sticks, wooden and plastic egg cups). Attach objects using string to a hanger What does the metal wind chimes sound like? How is the sound different from the wooden wind chimes? (KUW and CD) **Listening to the wind** Listen to the sound the wind makes through tubes of card and plastic as it whistles through. What happens to the sound if the tube is narrower? (KUW) **Paper Aeroplanes** Investigate, make and test which paper would make the best aeroplane. Which plane flew the furthest? Which plane stayed in the air the longest? (KUW and CD) **How strong is the wind?** Explore the strength of the wind using different materials and objects, e.g. feathers, stones, card, wood, metal and paper. Which objects moved or blew away in the wind? Which objects didn't move? Encourage the children to talk about what happened and why? (PSRN and KUW) **Wind painting** Using watered down ready mixed paint, place several drops onto a paper plate or sheet of paper. Place or hold the paper plate outside where the wind is able to catch the paint and create patterns. Alternatively use a straw and blow the paint around the paper plate. Encourage the children to look at the patterns and designs created and talk about them. (CD)

Appendix 7

Water tray Toy boats	**Washing line** Let the children wash dolls clothes and other clothing, then hang them out to dry on a line with pegs. Which clothes dried the quickest? What happened to the clothes when they were hanging on the line? (KUW and PSED) **Other activities** Make a flag. Make a parachute for a toy. Observe and talk about what happens to water as the wind blows it (e.g. ripples, waves) Make a sail for a toy boat and test in the water tray to see if it catches the wind and moves.

BOOKS

Kipper's Windy Day, Mick Inkpen *Kipper's Book of Weather*, Mick Inkpen *After the Storm*, Nick Butterworth *The Wind Blew*, Pat Hutchins *Titch's Windy Day*, Pat Hutchins *Alfie's Weather*, Shirley Hughes *Spot's Windy Day*, Eric Hill	*Elmer and the Wind*, David Mckee *Elmer's Weather*, David McKee *Maisie's Wonderful Weather Book*, Lucy Cousins *Warren and the Very Windy Day*, Liane Payne *The Windy Day*, Anna Milbourne *One Stormy Night*, Ruth Brown *Windy Days*, Jennifer S Burke

SONGS AND RHYMES

Let's go Fly a Kite Let's go fly a kite Up to the highest height Let's go fly a kite And send it soaring Up through the atmosphere Up where the air is clear Oh, let's go fly a kite. When you send it flying up there, All at once your lighter than air! You can dance on the breeze, Over houses and trees! With your fist holding tight, To the string of your kite!	**The Wind** The wind came out to play one day, He swept the clouds out of his way, He blew the leaves and away they flew, The trees bent low and their branches did too, The wind blew the great big ships at sea, The wind blew my kite away from me. **Clouds are floating** *(to the tune of 'Frere Jacques')* Clouds are floating, clouds are floating, Up so high, up so high, Floating up above us, floating up above us, In the sky, in the sky.

Activities for Frosty/Snowy Days

RESOURCES	ACTIVITIES
Snowy day clothing ● Coats ● All-in-one suits ● Scarves ● Woolly hats ● Gloves ● Wellington boots Mirrors Magnifying glasses Thermometer Photographs of snowflakes as seen under a microscope. (www.snowcrystals.com) **Make a snowflake** ● White paper ● Silver/gold paper ● Scissors **A selection of containers** ● Cups ● Trays (inc ice cube) ● Bowls ● Jelly moulds Food colouring Glitter Small toys (e.g. play mobile figures) Balloons Large empty sand tray Sand tools (spades, forks and buckets) Small world toys ● Vehicles (snow ploughs and sledges) ● Animals (polar bears, arctic foxes, seals, walruses, wolves and huskies) Trays with snow or ice Salt Sand Paintbrushes Sticks	**Snowflakes** Look closely at snowflakes, icicles and frost using magnifying glasses. Show the children photographs of real snowflakes close up and encourage them to talk about the shapes and patterns they can see? (KUW and PSRN) **Make a snowflake** Draw a circle shape onto a piece of white, silver or gold paper using a round object and cut out. Fold the circle in half three times until it looks like a slice of a pie. Hold the folded circle together and using the scissors cut out different shapes, patterns, swirls and spikes. (N.B. Don't cut too much of the folded edge). Unfold the circle and you have made your own 'unique' snowflake. (CD and PSRN) **Freezing water** Fill a selection of trays and containers with water and leave outside to freeze. Add food colouring, glitter, and other objects to the water. Watch what happens as the water freezes. Try filling balloons with water and leaving outside to freeze. (KUW) **Snow footsteps** Let the children enjoy walking in the frost or snow creating footsteps and listening to the crunching sounds they make. Encourage the children to play games, e.g. follow my footsteps - where children have to place their feet in the footsteps of the person in front of them without creating new footprints. (PSED) **Spider webs** Look for spider webs to observe how the frost and icicles have caught on the different threads and talk about the shapes and patterns they can see. (KUW and PSRN) **Snow play** If weather permitting you have had a fair amount of snow fall overnight it may be possible to collect and place in an empty sand tray for the children to play with. They can use sand tools, small world vehicles and animals to create an imaginary arctic environment. (CLL and PSED) **Effects of the cold on your body** Encourage the children to talk about what happens to their bodies when they are cold (i.e. goose bumps and misty breath). Give the children mirrors to observe what happens to their breath as they talk when they are outside. (PSED and KUW) **Melting snow** Show the children what happens to snow, frost or ice when you add salt or sand to it. Experiment using trays with snow or ice and encourage the children to watch what happens and talk about why and how the snow/ice melted. (KUW)

Appendix 7

Empty spray bottles Food colouring	**Snow writing** Give the children a stick or encourage them to use the end of a paintbrush to make scratching marks in the snow, frost or ice. (CLL) **Snow painting** Fill the spray bottles with cold water and add a few drops of food colouring so that you have bottles of red, blue, and yellow water. Be sure that the bottles have enough colouring in them to make them visible once they are sprayed on the snow. Let the children experiment and create pictures or patterns on the snow/frost by spraying the coloured water. (CD)

BOOKS

Kipper's Snowy Day, Mick Inkpen *Kipper's Book of Weather*, Mick Inkpen *Elmer in the Snow*, David McKee *Elmer's Weather*, David McKee *Titch's Snowy Day*, Pat Hutchins *Warren and the Snowy Day*, Liane Payne	*The Snowy Day*, Anna Milbourne *One Snowy Night*, Nick Butterworth *The Snowman*, Raymond Briggs *Alfie's Weather*, Shirley Hughes *Maisie's Wonderful Weather Book*, Lucy Cousins *Postman Pat's Snowy Delivery*, John Cunliffe

SONGS AND RHYMES

I'm a Little Snowflake *(to the tune of 'I'm a Little Teapot')* I'm a little snowflake, small and white. When the moon is shining I'm sparkly and bright. When you see me falling, Come out and play. You can make a snowman with me today.	**Fluffy Snowflakes** *(to the tune 'London Bridge is Falling Down')* Fluffy snowflakes falling down, falling down, falling down, fluffy snowflakes falling down, tickly, tingly snowflakes. **I'm a Little Snowman** *(to the tune of 'I'm a Little Teapot')* I'm a little Snowman, round and fat, I've got a woolly scarf and a little bobble hat. When the snow is falling, Come out and play. You can make a snowman with me today.

Activities for Sunny Days

RESOURCES	ACTIVITIES
Sunny day clothing ● Sun hats ● Sunglasses ● Shorts and T-shirts ● Flip flops ● Sandals ● Parasols	N.B. An important aspect of playing outside on sunny days is to develop children's awareness of 'sun safety'. **Shadows** Play games with puppets using hands or real objects. Can the children guess what they are? Play games with shadows. Can you chase your own shadow? What happens to your shadow as you move? (KUW)
Selection of different shaped objects Chalks	**Shadow drawing** Draw round the shadows created by different objects using chalks. Can the children match the objects to the shadows? Encourage the children to experiment with drawing round the shadows created by different-shaped objects. They may also have fun drawing round their friend's shadows. What will happen if they try to draw round their own shadow? (CD and KUW)
A stick with a weighted base Large sheet of paper Sealable plastic bags Black paper White paper Foil paper Coloured acetate sheets (red, blue and yellow)	**Sundials** Stand a stick in the centre of a large sheet of paper with a weight at the bottom to keep it in place. Draw round the shadow of the stick onto the paper and record the time of day using picture symbols. Continue to draw round the outline of the stick's shadow throughout the day choosing specific times that are meaningful to the children (e.g. register time, snack time, play time, lunchtime, assembly time, home time etc.). Discuss with the children what has happened to the stick's shadow during the day? What do they notice? Has the shadow moved? Has the shadow changed size? (PSRN and KUW)
Sunlight mobiles ● Hangers ● CDs ● Prisms ● Metal spoons ● Little mirrors ● Glass buttons ● Glass beads ● String	**How warm is the sun?** Fill several plastic bags with cold water and seal tightly. Cover each one with a different material: white paper, black paper and foil paper. Place the bags outside in the direct sunlight for a few hours and then open them to test the warmth of the water inside. Which bag will have the warmest water? Why? (KUW)
Bubbles Washing line and pegs Washing up bowl Selection of dolls clothes	**Coloured glasses** Encourage the children to look at objects outside using coloured acetate sheets (e.g. trees, birds, grass, buildings etc.). What do they notice? Experiment with different colours. What happens to the colours of objects if they look through the yellow and blue acetate sheets together? (CD and PSRN)
Role-play area ● A selection of sun hats ● A selection of sun glasses ● T-shirts ● Shorts ● Swimming costumes ● Goggles ● Snorkelling gear ● Flip flops ● Sandals ● Arm bands ● Deck chairs ● Tent	**Sunlight mobiles** Hang a selection of shiny and glass objects to a hanger or a tree branch and encourage the children to watch what happens as the sun reflects off them or shines on them. (KUW)

Appendix 7

Water tray with water toys Sand tray with sand toys Tarpaulins or sheets to make dens Selection of mark-making tools and implements	**Bubbles** Children love playing with bubbles whatever the weather, but on sunny days it is particularly fun to watch the bubbles as the sunlight reflects through them creating rainbows. Can the children catch the bubbles and pop them before they float away? Who can blow the biggest bubble? Who can blow a different-shaped bubble? (PSRN, KUW and CD) **Washing line** Let the children wash dolls clothes and other clothing, then hang them out to dry on a line with pegs. Which clothes dried the quickest? What happened to the clothes when they were hanging on the line? (KUW and PSED) **Role-play** Create a holiday resort with dressing up clothes and sunny day props for the children to play imaginatively with. (PSED and CLL) **Other activities** Create a shady area or build a den. Sand and water play Mark-making using chalks, paintbrushes and water pots

BOOKS

Hot Days, Jennifer S Burke *Sunny Days*, Jennifer S Burke *Kipper's Sunny Day*, Mick Inkpen *Kipper's Book of Weather*, Mick Inkpen	*The Sunny Day*, Anna Milbourne *Elmer and the Rainbow*, David McKee *Elmer's Weather*, David McKee *Maisie's Wonderful Weather Book*, Lucy Cousins *Alfie's Weather*, Shirley Hughes

SONGS AND RHYMES

I am Sun Safe *(to the tune 'Old MacDonald had a Farm')* I am sun-safe all day long, Ee ii ee ii oo I wear a hat to shade my face. Ee ii ee ii oo With a floppy hat here, And a floppy hat there, here a hat, there a hat, Everywhere a floppy hat, I am sun-safe all day long, Ee ii ee ii oo Repeat song with additional sentences 'I wear sunglasses to protect my eyes' 'With dark glasses here....etc' 'I wear sun cream on my body' 'With sun cream here...etc 'I sit down under a shady spot' 'With a shady spot here...etc'	**The Sun has got his hat on** The sun has got his hat on Hip-hip-hip-hooray! The sun has got his hat on, He's coming out to play. Now we'll all be happy, Hip-hip-hip-hooray! The sun has got his hat on, And he's coming out today. **Rainbow Song** Red and yellow and pink and green, Purple and orange and blue. I can sing a rainbow, Sing a rainbow, Sing a rainbow too!

Activities for Foggy Days

RESOURCES	ACTIVITIES
Foggy day clothing ● Coats ● Scarves ● Gloves ● Reflective vests or tabards Selection of torches with powerful beams Mirrors **High visibility materials** ● Reflective arm bands ● Reflective badges ● Reflective stickers ● Silver foil ● Luminous objects ● White paper Luminous paint Luminous felt pens **Glow-in-the-dark objects** ● Necklaces ● Bracelets ● Sticks ● Stickers **Make fog** ● Glass jar ● Strainer ● Water ● Ice cubes	**Role-play** Set up an emergency department role-play with police, ambulance and fire fighters. Use dressing up costumes with reflective vests/tabards and include lighting on bikes and other vehicles. Ask the children to think about roads and runways and how they can be seen in the fog? e.g. 'Cat's eyes'. (PSED, CLL and PD) **Torch lights** Encourage the children to experiment with different types of torches. Stand a certain distance away from each other and use the torch by flashing it. What happens to the light when the torch is switched on in the fog? Can the other person see the light through the fog? How many flashes can they count? (KUW and PSRN) **Hide and seek** Put reflective bands or badges on and stand a certain distance away from each other. Use the torch to find their friend and see if the light reflects off the badge or band to show them where they are. (KUW) **Luminous painting** Use luminous paints and felt pens to draw pictures or warning signs for the role-play area. Which colours are easiest to see in the fog/dark? (CD) **Reflective objects** Explore which objects reflect the light using the torch to test them in the fog. (KUW) **Make your own fog** Fill up the jar completely with hot water and leave for about a minute. Pour out almost all the water but leave about 3cm in the jar. Put the strainer over the opening at the top of the jar. Place 3 or 4 ice cubes in the strainer. Encourage the children to watch the jar closely and talk about what happens. The cold air from the ice cubes mixes with the warm moist air in the jar and forms an eerie fog. (KUW)
BOOKS	
Postman Pat's Foggy Day, John Cunliffe *Cloudy Days*, Jennifer S Burke *Kipper's Book of Weather*, Mick Inkpen	*Elmer's Weather*, David McKee *Maisie's Wonderful Weather Book*, Lucy Cousins *Alfie's Weather*, Shirley Hughes
SONGS AND RHYMES	
The Fog I like the fog It's soft and cool, It hides everything On the way to school. I can't see a house I can't see a tree, Because the fog Is playing with me. The sun comes out The fog goes away, But it shall be back Another day.	**A Foggy Day** When I go outside and look around, It seems like there's a cloud on the ground. It's hard to see, everything is grey, It's a foggy day. Be careful move slow, Everywhere you go. Like a blanket from the sky, A foggy day for you and I.

Some challenges for boys

- Go on a scavenger hunt and find materials to replace paint brushes.
- Try ice cube painting and dyeing.
- Make a play dough monster or your favourite foods.
- Use tongs, pegs, clips and a hole punch to make a den.
- Make a themed puppet to link with a book.
- Make an 'Angry Birds' fruit salad.
- Make a Pringle Piñata of core words.
- Create a structure with raisins and tooth picks.
- Make hot car wax crayons.
- Take a bug or a car for a paint drive.
- Create a salt ice sculpture.
- Erupt a sand volcano.
- Jump back with paint bombs.
- Use an OHP to create monster bugs.
- Joust as knights on space hoppers.

Particular schemas that flourish outdoors

Transporting

This is when a child is interested in moving around, transporting objects from one place to another. Practitioners need to provide wheeled toys plus equipment such as bags, buckets, baskets and containers to move things from place to place plus other equipment to move through space in different ways plus a variety of containers to transport. These children will enjoy picnics, emptying or filling the paddling pool too.

Trajectory

This is when a child is interested in how objects and people move, and how they can affect that movement. Practitioners should be prepared for very active and vigorous learning as these children often have very good physical skills via jumping, swinging, sliding, repeated throwing and climbing up and down. A range of different types of blocks, ladders, slides, climbing equipment, balls, hoops, tyres as well as smaller resources to cut, bang, tear, saw, flick etc. via a range of creative activities such as spray and splatter painting and woodwork.

Connecting

This is when a child shows an interest in fastening things together as well as taking them apart. Practitioners need to provide resources such as train tracks, threading, model building and string, tape and rope extensions with lots of wool, ribbon, string and tape plus the resources to connect so these children can explore how different things can be joined together in different ways. Children interested in connecting particularly enjoy the opportunity to deconstruct old machines and technology as well as a collection of zips and fasteners.

Rotation

This is when a child develops an interest in things which turn, such as knobs, keys, taps and wind-up toys. They may also run round in circles often getting dizzy or make circular or spiral type drawings. They need space to play circle games, push wheelbarrows and buggies around, spin umbrellas or the open parachute, spin Sycamore keys, unwind and rewind the hose, spin hoops, balls and wheels both large and small.

Enveloping/enclosing

This is when a child becomes interested in creating and/or occupying enclosed spaces. Some spaces may be full or empty and such children are interested in ownership. Thus practitioners should provide open-ended resources so children can hide away inside cardboard boxes, under fabric pieces as well as small resources such as a selection of bags and boxes for hiding away smaller items. Farm and wild animals with materials to make enclosures are popular, as is hiding under the table!

Bibliography

Abbott, L. and Nutbrown, C. (2001) *Experiencing Reggio Emilia: Implications For Pre-School Provision.* Buckingham: Open University Press.

Abbott, L. and Rodger, R. (1994) *Quality Education in the Early Years.* Buckingham: Open University Press.

Alexander, T. (1997) *Family Learning: The Foundations of Effective Education.* London: DEMOS.

Athey, C. (1990) *Extending Thought in Young Children: A Parent–Teacher Partnership.* London: Paul Chapman Publishing.

Bailey, R. (1999) 'Play, health and physical development', in T. David (Ed.) *Young Children Learning.* London: Paul Chapman Publishing.

Baker-Graham, A. (1994) 'Can outdoor education encourage creative learning opportunities?' *Journal of Outdoor and Adventure Education* 40(11): 23–25.

Ball, C. (Ed.) (1994) *Start Right: The Importance of Early Learning.* London: Royal Society for the Encouragement of Arts, Manufacture and Commerce.

Ball, D. (2002) *Risks, Benefits and Choices.* HSE Books: Middlesex University.

Ball, D. (2004) 'Policy issues and risk-benefit trade-offs of "safer surfacing" for children's playgrounds.' *Accident Analysis and Prevention* 35(4): 417–42.

Ballantyne, R., Connell, S., and Fien, J. (1998) 'Students as a catalyst of environmental change: a framework for researching inter-generational influence through environmental education.' *Environmental Education Research* 4(3): 285–98.

Barber, M. (1996) *The Learning Game.* London: Victor Gollancz.

Barnes, P. (2000) *Values and Outdoor Learning.* Penrith: Association for Outdoor Learning.

Bates, B. (1996) 'Like rats in a rage.' *Times Educational* Supplement, 20 September.

Belle Beard, L. (2007) *An Outdoor Book for Girls.* Stroud: The History Press.

Bennett, N. and Kell, J. (1989) *A Good Start? Four Year Olds in Infants' School.* Oxford: Blackwell.

Bennett, N., Wood, L. and Rogers, S. (1997) *Teaching Through Play: Teachers Thinking and Classroom Practice.* Buckingham: Open University Press.

Beodie, P. (1995) 'Where are the risk takers in outdoor education? A critical analysis of two current perspectives.' *Adventure Education and Outdoor Living* 12(4).

Berry, M. and Hodgson, C. (Eds) (2011) *Adventure Education.* Abingdon: Routledge.

Bibliography

Biddle, S. and Biddle, G. (1989) cited in Bailey, R. (1999) 'Play, health and physical development', in T. David (Ed.) *Young Children Learning*. London: Paul Chapman Publishing.

Biddulph, S. (2008) *Raising Boys*. London: Harper Thomas.

Bilton, H. (2002) *Outdoor Play in the Early Years*. London: David Fulton Publishers.

Bixler, R.D., Floyd, M.E. and Hammutt, W.E. (2002) 'Environmental socialization: qualitative tests of the childhood play hypothesis.' *Environment and Behaviour*, 34(6): 795–18.

Boniface, M. (2000) 'Towards an understanding of flow and other positive experience phenomena within outdoor and adventurous activities.' *Journal of Adventure Education and Outdoor Learning*, 1(1): 55–68.

Boyce, E.R. (1938) *Play In The Infants' School: An Account Of An Educational Experiment At The Raleigh Infants' School, Stepney, London, January 1933–April 1936*. London: Methuen.

Bradford Education (1995) *Can I Play Outdoors? Outdoor Play in the Early Years*. Bradford: Bradford Education.

Bridgewater College (2004) *Forest School: A Classroom Without Walls. 10 Years of Leading the Way*. Available at: www.bridgewater.ac.uk/forestschool.

Broughton, H. (1915) *The Open Air School*. London: Pitman.

Brown, A.L. and Kane, M.J. (1988) 'Pre school children can learn to transfer: learning to learn and learning from example.' *Cognitive Psychology* 20(4): 493–523.

Brown. F. and Webb, S. (2005) 'Children without play.' *Journal of Education*, 35(March).

Bruce, T. (1991) *Time to Play in Early Childhood Education*. London: Hodder and Stoughton.

Bruce, T. (2004) *Early Childhood Education*, 2nd edition. London: Hodder and Stoughton.

Brunner, J.S. (1961) 'The act of discovery.' *Harvard Educational Review*, 31(1): 21–32.

Brunner, J.S. (1974) *Relevance of Education*. Harmondsworth: Penguin.

Brunner, J.S. (1977) 'Differences between experiential and classroom learning', in M.T. Keeton (Ed.) *Experiential Learning: Rationale, Characteristics and Assessment*. San Francisco: Jossey-Boss.

Carson, R. (1999) *The Sense of Wonder*. London: Harper Collins.

Child Alert (n.d.) 'Safety.' Available at: www.childalert.co.uk/safety.php?tab=Safety

Church, G.W. (2000) 'Field trips and developmental education.' *Inquiry* 5(1): 32–36.

Clarke, J. (2007) *Sustained Shared Thinking*. London: Featherstone.

Claxton, G. (1990) *Teaching to Learn: A Direction for Education*. London: Cassell.

Clemens, S.G. (1999) *Editing: Permission to Start Wrong*. London: Caddell.

Clouder, C. and Rawson, M. (1998) *Waldorf Education*. Edinburgh: Floris Books.

Cobb, E. (1977) *The Ecology of Imagination in Childhood*. New York: Columbia University Press.

Community Playthings with Scott, W. (2011) *Lighting The Fire: Hands-on Investigation, Play and Outdoor Learning in Primary Education*. Robertsbridge: Community Products (UK) Limited.

Cook, B. and Heseltine, P.J. (1998) *Assessing Risk on Children's Playgrounds* (2nd edition). Birmingham: ROSPA.

Cook, T. and Hess. E. (2005) 'Children's voices.' Paper developed from Sure Start Early Excellence Evaluation. Newcastle: Northumbria University.

Cornell, J. (1984) *Sharing Nature with Children.* Watford: Exley.

Cornell, J. (1987) *Listening to Nature: How to Deepen Your Awareness of Nature.* Watford: Exley.

Cosco, N. (2005) *Environmental Interventions for Healthy Development of Young Children in the Outdoors.* Open Space, People Space Conference, 19–21 September 2007, Edinburgh. Available at: http://www.openspace.eca.ac.uk/conference/proceedingd?PDF/Cosco.pdf

Crebbin, C. (1997) There is no bad weather – just bad clothing: Swedish environmental education in the early years.' *Environmental Education, Journal of the National Association for Environmental Education (UK),* 55(Summer): 7–8.

Crook, S. and Farmer, B. (1996) *Just Imagine: Creative Play Experiences for Children Under Six.* Melbourne: RMIT Publishing.

Csikszentmihalyi, M. (1997) *Finding Flow: The Psychology of Engagement with Everyday Life.* New York: Basic Books.

Cullen, J. (1993) 'Pre school children's use and perceptions of outdoor play areas.' *Early Childhood Development and Care,* 89: 45–56.

Danks, F. and Scofield, J. (2005) *Nature's Playground.* London: Francis Lincoln.

Davies, J. (1991) 'Children's adjustment to nursery class: how to equalise opportunities for a successful experience.' *School Organisation,* 11(3): 255–62.

Davies, J. and Brember, I. (1991) 'The effects of gender and attendance on children's adjustment to nursery classes.' *British Educational Research Journal,* 17(1): 73–82.

Davies, N. (1939) *Ten Years History of the Chelsea Open Air Nursery School.* London: COAN.

Department for Children, Schools and Families (2008) S*tatutory Framework for the Early Years Foundation Stage: Setting the Standards for Learning, Development and Care for Children from Birth to Five* (revised edition). London: Department for Children, Schools and Families Publications.

Department for Education (DfES) (2007) *Statutory Framework for the Early Years Foundation Stage EYFS-Every Child Matters.* London: Department for Education.

Department for Education (2008) 'Early Years Foundation Stage (EYFS)'. Available at: http://webarchive.nationalarchives.gov.uk/20130401151715/http://www.education.gov.uk/publications/standard/publicationDetail/Page1/DCSF-00261-2008

Department for Education (2012) *Development Matters in the Early Years Foundation Stage: Non Statutory Guidance Material Supports Practitioners in Implementing the Statutory Requirements of the Early Years Foundation Stage* (revised edition). London: Department for Education.

Derr, V. (2002) 'Children's sense of place in Northern New Mexico.' *Journal of Environmental Psychology,* 22(1-2): 125–37.

Dewey, J. (1867) 'My pedagocical creed', *The School Journal,* LIV: 3.

Dewey, J. (1938) *Experience and Education.* New York: Macmillan.

Douglas, M. (1992) *Risk and Blame: Essays in Cultural Theory.* London: Routledge.

Dunkin, D. and Hanna, P. (2001) *Thinking Together: Quality Adult–Child Interactions.* Wellington, New Zealand: NZCER Press.

Bibliography

Dweck, C.S. (2000) *Self-Theories: Their Role in Motivation, Personality and Development.* Philadelphia: Psychology Press.

Edgington, M. (2002) *The Great Outdoors.* London: BAECE.

Education Scotland (2004) 'Early Years Vision and Values for Outdoor Play'. Available at: http://www.educationscotland.gov.uk/Images/Vision_and_Values_for_Outdoor_Play_tcm4-597073.pdf

Elkind, D. (1987) *Miseducation: Preschoolers at Risk.* New York: Knopf.

Elkind, D. (2007) *The Power of Play.* Philadelphia: Lifelong Books, Da Capo Press.

EPPE (2001) 'The Effective Provision of Pre-School Education Project (EPPE), A longitudinal study funded by the DfEE (1997-2003).' Available at: www.ioe.ac.uk/schools/ecpe/eppe/eppe

Falk, J. and Dierking, L. (1992) *The Museum Experience.* Washington, DC: Whalesback Books.

Featherstone, S. and Bayley, R. (2005) *Boys and Girls Come Out to Play.* Leicestershire: Featherstone Education Ltd.

Feinburg, S. and Minders, M. (1994) *Eliciting Children's Full Potential.* California: Wadsworth.

Fields, J.I. (1993) 'Primary perspectives: the supporting role of economic and industrial understanding.' *Early Childhood Development and Care*, 94: 5–9.

Fjortoft, I. and Sageie, J. (2000) 'The natural environment as a playground for children: landscape description and analysis of a natural landscape.' *Landscape and Urban Planning*, 48(1/2): 83–97.

Fjortoft, I. (2004) 'Landscape as playscape: the effects of natural environments on children's play and motor development.' *Children, Youth and Environments*, 14(20): 21–27.

Ford, P. (1981) *Principles and Practices of Outdoor Environmental Education.* New York: Wiley and Sons.

Froebel, F. (1887) *The Education of Man.* Translated by Hailmann, W.N. New York/London: D. Appleton Century.

Fulbrook, J. (2005) *Outdoor Activities, Negligence and the Law.* Aldershot: Ashgate Publishing.

Furedi, F. (2002) *Culture of Fear: Risk Taking And The Morality Of Low Expectations.* London: Continuum.

Furstenberg, F.F. with Cherlin, A.J. (1988) *The New American Grandparent: A Place in the Family, a Life Apart.* New York: Basic Books.

Gambell, S. and Hasan, B. (2011) 'Rise to the challenge.' *Nursery World*, 29 November, 26–27.

Garrick, R. (2004) *Playing Outdoors in the Early Years.* London: Continuum.

Gill, T. (2006) 'Home zones in the UK: history, policy and impact on children and youth.' *Children, Youth and Environments*, 16: 90–103.

Gill, T. (2007) *No Fear: Growing Up In A Risk Adverse Society.* London: Calouste Gulbenkian Foundation.

Gill, T. (2009) 'Now for free-range childhood.' *Guardian*, 2 April. Available at: www.guardian.co.uk/commentisfree/2009/apr/02/children-safety

Gill, T. (2010) 'Nothing ventured: balancing risks and benefits in the outdoors.' The English Outdoor Council. Available at: www.englishoutdoorcouncil.org.

Gleave, J. (2008) 'Risk and Play: A Literature Review'. London: Play England. Available at: www.playday.org.uk/PDF/Risk-and-play-a-literature-review.pdf.

Gleave, J. and Cole-Hamilton, I. (2012) 'A World Without Play: A Literature Review.' Available at: www.playengland.org.uk/media/371031/a-world-without-play-literature-review-2012.pdf.

Goddard Blythe, S.A. (2000) 'First steps to the most important A, B, C' *Times Educational Supplement*, 7 January.

Goddard Blythe, S.A. (2003) *The Well Balanced Child: Movement and Early Learning.* Stroud: Hawthorn Press.

Goddard Blythe, S.A. (2005) 'Releasing educational potential through movement: A summary of individual studiers using the INPP Test Battery and Development Programme for use in Schools.' *Child Care in Practice*, 11(4): 415–32.

Goddard Blythe, S.A. (2009) *Attention, Balance and Co-ordination: The A,B,C of Learning Success.* Chichester: Wiley-Blackwell.

Goddard Blythe, S.A. (2011) *The Right to Move: Assessing Neuromotor Readiness for Learning. Why physical development in the early years supports educational success.* Based upon a verbal presentation given to the Quality of Childhood Group in the European Parliament in May 2011 by Sally Goddard Blythe hosted by MEP Edward McMillan Scott.

Goddard Blythe, S.A. (2012) 'Assessing neuromotor readiness for learning.' Available at: http://sallygoddardblythe.co.uk/12th-april-2012-publication-of-assessing-neuromotor-readiness-for-learning/

Goldschmied, E. and Jackson, S. (2004) *People Under Three* (2nd edition). Abingdon: Routledge.

Goswami, U. (2004) 'Neuroscience, education and special education'. *British Journal of Special Education*, 31(4): 175–83.

Grahn, P., Martensson, F., Llindblad, B., Nilsson, P. and Ekman, A. (1997) UTE pa DAGIS, Stad & Land nr. 93/1991 Sveriges lantbruksuniversitet, Alnarp.

Greenman, J. (1988) *Caring Spaces, Learning Places.* Redmond, WA: Exchange Press Inc.

Groves, L. and McNish, H. (2008) *Baseline Study of Play at Merrylee Primary School, Glasgow.* Edinburgh: Forestry Commission.

Haddow Report (1933) *Infant and Nursery Schools.* London: HMSO.

Hammernan, D. and Priest, S. (1989) 'Outdoor education begins with the opening of the classroom window.' *Journal of Outdoor and Adventure Education*, 1(3).

Harden, J. (2000) 'There's no place like home.' *Childhood*, 7(1): 43–59.

Hassett, J.D. and Weisberg, A. (1972) *Open Education: Alternatives within Our Tradition.* Upper Saddle River, NJ: Prentice Hall.

Hawke, D. (1991) 'Field trips and how to get the most out of them.' *Pathways*, 3(2): 16–17.

Hawkins, C. (2010) 'Inflated view of risk inhibits children.' *Nursery World*: 11 November.

Health and Safety Executive (1997) Infection risks to new and expectant mothers in the workplace. Available at: http://www.hse.gov.uk?pubns/priced/infection-mothers.pdf.

Bibliography

Health and Safety Executive (2006) 'HSC tells health and safety pedants to "get a life": statement by Bill Callaghan, Chair of the Health and Safety Commission.' Available at: www.hse.gov.uk/risk/statement.htm.

Health and Safety Executive (2007) RSA Risk Commission Conference (31 October, 2007). Available at: www.hse.gov.uk/AboutHSE.

Health and Safety Executive (2011) 'School trips and outdoor learning activities: Tackling the health and safety myths.' Available at: http://www.hse.gov.uk/services/education/school-trips.pdf

Health and Safety Executive (2014) 'Risk.' Available at: www.hse.gov.uk/risk.

Health and Safety Executive (2014) 'Young people, risk and an exciting education.' Available at: www.hse.gove.uk/news/judith-risk-assessment/youngpeople300312.htm.

Heerwagen, J.H. and Oriens, G.H. (2002) 'The ecological world of children.' In Kahn, P. and Kellert, S. (Eds) *Children and Nature*. Cambridge, MA: MIT Press.

Hendy, L. and Whitebread, D. (2000) 'Interpretations of independent learning in the early years.' *International Journal of Early Years Education*, 8(3): 243–52.

Hernandez, K. (2007) 'The pros and cons of risk taking behaviour in children.' Available at: http://www.parenthood360.com/index.php/the-pros-and-cons-of-risk-taking-behavior-in-children-3-31003/

Hopkins, D. (1982) 'Self-concept and adventure: the process of change.' *Adventure Education* 2(1): 7–13.

Hurtwood, Lady Allen of. (1968) *Planning for Play*. London: Thames and Hudson.

Hutt, S.J., Tyler, S., Hutt, C. and Christopherson, H. (1989) *Play, Exploration and Learning: A Natural History of the Pre-School*. London: Routledge.

Iggulden, C. and Iggulden, H. (2006) *The Dangerous Book for Boys*. London: Harper Collins.

IPSOS MORI Social Research Institute (2011) 'Children's Well-being in UK, Sweden and Spain: The Role of Inequality and Materialism.' 14 September, 2011. Available at: www.ipsos-mori.com.

Isaacs, B. (2007) *Bringing the Montessori Approach to your Early Years Practice*. Abingdon: Routledge.

Isaacs, S. (1930) *Intellectual Growth in Young Children*. London: Routledge.

Isaacs, S. (1932) *The Children We Teach: Seven to Eleven Years*. London: University of London Press.

Isaacs, S. (1936 [1931]) *Intellectual Growth in Young Children*. London: Routledge and Kegan Paul.

Isaacs, S. (1948) *Childhood and After: Some Essays and Clinical Studies*. [Reprinted 1999] London: Routledge.

Isaacs, S. (1951 [1933]) *Social Development in Young Children*. London: Routledge.

Isaacs, S. (1952). 'The nature and function of phantasy'. In M. Klein, P. Heimann, S. Isaacs, & J. Riviere (Eds), *Developments in Psycho-analysis*, 43: 67–121. London: Hogarth Press.

Isaacs, S. (1954) *The Educational Value of the Nursery School*. London: The Nursery Association of Great Britain and Northern Ireland (Reprinted by BAECE, London).

Kagan, J. (1994) *The Nature of the Child*. London: Basic Books.

Kahn, P.H. and Kellert, S.R. (2002) *Children and Nature: Psychological, Sociocultural and Evolutionary Investigations.* Boston: MIT Press.

Kelmer-Pringle, M. (1973) *The Roots of Violence and Vandalism.* London: The National Children's Bureau.

Keyes, R. (1985) *Chancing It. Why We Take Risks.* Boston: Little, Brown and Co.

KIDS (2008) *In All of Us: The Framework for Quality Inclusion.* Available at: www.kids.org.uk.

Knight, S. (2011) *Risk and Adventure in Early Years Outdoor Play: Learning From Forest Schools.* London: SAGE.

Kostelnik, M.J., Whiten, A.P. and Stein, L.C. (1986) 'Living with He-man: managing super-hero fantasy play.' *Young Children,* 41(4): 3–9.

Kritchevsky, S. and Prescott, E., with Walling, L. (1977). *Planning Environments For Young Children: Physical Space* (2nd edition). Washington DC: NAEYC, p. 5.

Kytta, M. (2006) 'Environmental child-friendliness in the light of the Bullerby model.' In C. Spencer and M. Blades (Eds), *Children and their Environments: Learning, Using and Designing Spaces.* Cambridge: Cambridge University Press.

Laevers, F., Daems, M., De Bruyckere, G., Declercq, B., Moons, J., Silkens, K., Snoeck, G. and Van Kessel, M. (2005) *Well-being and Involvement in Care: A Process Orientated Self-evaluation Instrument for Care Settings.* Leuven University, Belgium: Centre for Experiential Education. Available at: www.kindengezin.be/Images/Zikohand leidingENG_tcm149-50761.pdf.

Lally, M. (1991) *The Nursery Teacher in Action.* London: Paul Chapman Publishing.

Liebschner, J. (1992) *A Child's Work: Freedom and Guidance in Froebel's Education Theory and Practice.* Cambridge: Butterworth Press.

Lindon, J. (1999) *Too Safe for Their Own Good? Helping Children Learn about Risk and Lifeskills.* London: National Children's Bureau.

London Sustainable Development Commission (2011) 'Sowing the seeds: reconnecting London's children with nature.' Available at: http://www.londonsdc.org/documents/Sowing%20the%20Seeds%20-%20Full%20Report.pdf.

Loughborough University (2012) 'Make time to play: the impact of toys and play on children's physical activity.' In conjunction with the Institute of Youth Sport, Loughborough University and the Toy and Hobby Association. Available at: www.maketime2play.org.uk.

Louv, R. (1991) *Childhood's Future.* New York: Doubleday.

Louv, R. (2005) *Last Child in the Woods.* New York, Chapel Hill: Algonquin Books.

Lucas, B. and Claxton, G. (2010) *New Kinds of Smart.* Maidenhead: Open University Press.

McMillan, M. (1930) *The Nursery School.* London: Dent and Sons.

Mental Health Foundation. (1999) *Bright Futures: Promoting Children and Young People's Mental Health.* London: Mental Health Foundation.

Millard, E. (2010) 'Responding to gender difference.' In J. Arthur & T. Cremin (Eds) *Learning to Teach in the Primary School* 2nd edition. London: Routledge.

Montessori, M. (1912) *The Montessori Method: Scientific Pedagogy as Applied to Child Education in the Children's Houses.* New York: Frederick A. Stokes Company.

Bibliography

Mooney, A. and Blackburn, T. (2003) *Children's Views on Childcare Quality*. DfES Research Report RR482. London: HMSO.

Moore, R.C. (1986) 'The power of nature: orientations of girls and boys towards biotic and abiotic play settings on a reconstructed schoolyard.' *Children's Environments Quarterly*, 3(3).

Moore, R.C. (1996) 'Compact nature: the role of playing and learning gardens on children's lives.' *Journal of Therapeutic Horticulture*, 8: 72–82.

Moore, R.C. and Wong, H. (1997) *Natural Learning: The Life History Of An Environmental Schoolyard: Creating Environments For Rediscovering Nature's Way Of Teaching*. Berkeley: MIG Communications.

Moll, L.C. (Ed.) (1990 reprinted 1994) *Vygotsky and Education*. Cambridge: Cambridge University Press.

Mortlock, C. (1994) *The Adventure Alternative*. Cumbria: Cicerone Press.

Mortlock, C. (2009) *The Spirit of Adventure*. Kendal: Outdoor Integrity Publishing.

Moss, S. (2012) *Natural Childhood*. National Trust. Available at: www.outdoornation@nationaltrust.org.uk.

Moylett, H. and Stewart, N. (2012) *Understanding the Revised Early Years Foundation Stage*. London: BAECE.

Nairn, A. (2011) *Children's Well-being in UK, Sweden and Spain: The Role of Inequality and Materialism*. Bath: Ipsos MORI Social Research Institute.

National Health Service (2009) 'Health Survey for England – 2008: physical activity and fitness-volume 1'. Available at: www.ic.nhs.uk/pubs/hse08physicalactivity.

National Health Service (2010) 'Statistics on obesity, physical activity and diet: England 2012'. Available at: www.ic.nhs.uk/webfiles/publications/opad10/Statistics_on Obesity_Physical_Activity_and_Diet_England_2012.pdf.

National Institute for Health and Care Excellence (2009) 'Promoting physical activity for children and young people'. Available at: http://www.nice.org.uk/guidance/ph17/chapter/introduction.

National Playing Fields Association (2000) *Best Play: What Play Provision Should do for Children*. London: NPFA/ Children's Play Council/PLAYLINK.

National Schools Partnership (2012) 'Arla: We helped Arla win awards for their "Closer to Nature" brand change campaign.' Available at: http://agency.nationalschoolspartnership.com/case-studies/arla/.

National Trust (2012) '50 things to do before you're 11 ¾.' Available at: www.50things.org.uk.

Natural England (2009) 'Childhood and nature: a survey on changing relationships with nature across generations.' Available at: www.naturalengland.org.uk/Images/Childhood%20%%20Nature%20Survey_tcm6-10515.pdf.

New Zealand Ministry of Education. (1996) *Te Whariki Early Education Childhood Curriculum*. Wellington: Learning Media.

Nicol, J. (2007) *Bringing the Steiner Waldorf Approach to Your Early Years Practice*. Abingdon: Routledge.

Nobel. C., Brown, J. and Murphy, J. (2001) *How to Raise Boys' Achievement*. London: David Fulton Publications.

Nutbrown, C. (2001) *Threads of Thinking: Young Children Learning and the Role of Early Education.* London: Sage.

O'Brien, L. (2005a) *Trees and Woodlands: Nature's Health Service.* London: Forest Research.

O'Brien, L. (2005b) *Trees and Their Impact on the Emotional Well-being of Local Residents on Two Inner London Social Housing Estates.* London: Forest Research.

O'Brien, L. and Murray, R. (2007) 'Forest school and its impact on young children: case studies in Britain.' *Urban Forestry and Urban Greening,* 6(2): 49–65.

Ofsted. (2008) 'Learning outside the classroom.' Available at: www.ofsted.gov.uk/resources/learning-outside-classroom.

Ouvry, M. (2005) *Exercising Muscles and Minds: Outdoor Play and the Early Years Curriculum.* London: National Children's Bureau.

Oxford University Press Compact Dictionary Online (2011). Available at: www.oed.com.

Parkin, J. (1997) 'Boys and girls come out to play.' *Times Educational Supplement Extra,* 13: June, VI.

Parsons, C. (1995) 'Field trips can enhance family involvement.' *Dimensions of Early Childhood,* 23(4): 16–18.

Payley, V.G. (1984) *Boys and Girls: Superheros in the Doll Corner.* Chicago: University of Chicago Press.

Payley, V.G. (1988) *Bad Guys Don't Have Birthdays: Fantasy Play at Four.* Chicago: The University of Chicago Press.

Pellegrini, A.D. (2005) *The Role of Recess in Children's Cognitive Performance and School Adjustment: Educational Researcher.* Mahwah, NJ: Lawrence Erlbaum Associates.

Pellegrini, A.D. and Smith, P.K. (1998) 'Physical activity play: the nature and function of a neglected aspect of play.' *Child Development,* 69(3): 577–98.

Play England (2012) 'Children missing out on great outdoors.' Available at: www.playengland.org.uk/news/2012/08/children_missing_out_on_the_great_outdoors.aspx.

Playnotes (2008) 'Boys and the outdoors (November): curriculum support risk assessments.' Available to members of Learning Through Landscapes. Available at: www.ltl.org.uk.

Playnotes (2009) 'Up, over and under (July): curriculum support risk assessments.' Available to members of Learning Through Landscapes. Available at: www.ltl.org.uk.

Playnotes (2010) 'Nooks and crannies (September): curriculum support risk assessments.' Available to members of Learning Through Landscapes. Available at: www.ltl.org.uk.

Playnotes (2011) 'Adventurous play (January): curriculum support risk assessments.' Available to members of Learning Through Landscapes. Available at: www.ltl.org.uk.

Plowden Report (1967) *Children and Their Primary Schools: A Report of the Central Advisory Council for Education (England) Volume I Report.* London: HMSO.

Priest, S. (1991) 'The ten commandments of adventure education', *Journal of Adventure Education and Outdoor Leadership,* 8: 8–10.

Pyle, R. (2002) 'Eden in a vacant lot: special places, species and kids in community life.' In: P.H. Kahn and S.R. Kellert (Eds) *Children and Nature: Psychological, Sociocultural and Evolutionary Investigations.* Cambridge, MA: MIT Press.

Bibliography

Roemmich, J.N., Epstein, L.H., Raja, S. and Lin, Y. (2007) 'The neighbourhood and home environments: disparate relationships with physical activity and sedentary behaviours in youth.' *Annals of Behavioural Medicine*, 33(1): 29–38.

Royal Society for the Prevention of Accidents (1995) Poisonous plants: a set of three posters. *Take Care! Be Plant Aware*. Bristol: RoSPA.

Royal Society for the Prevention of Accidents (2008) 'RoSPA child accident statistics.' Available at: www.rospa.com.

Royal Society for the Prevention of Accidents (2010) 'Advice on outdoor risks.' Available at: http://www.rospa.com/schoolandcollegesafety/teachingsafely/governmentstake holderadvice/outdoor-risk-advice.aspx.

Royal Society for the Prevention of Accidents (2014) 'Are playgrounds safe? Frequently asked questions.' Available at: www.rospa.com/faqs.

Royal Society for the Protection of Birds (2013) *State of Nature Report*. Available at: http://www.rspb.org.uk/Images/stateofnature_tcm9-345839.pdf.

Sandberg, A. and Pramling-Samuelson, I. (2005) 'An interview study of gender differences in preschool teachers' attitudes towards children's play.' *Early Childhood Education Journal*, 32(5): 297–305.

Santer, J. and Griffiths, C., with Goodall, D. (2007) *Free Play in Early Childhood*. London: National Children's Bureau.

Scholfield, J. and Danks, F. (2012) *The Stick Book*. London: Frances Lincoln.

Sigman, A. (2007) *Agricultural Literacy: Giving Concrete Children Food For Thought*. Available at: www.face-online.org.uk/resources/news/Agricultura&20Literacy.pdf.

Siraj-Blatchford, I. (2001) 'Diversity and learning in the early years.' In G. Pugh (Ed.) *Contemporary Issues in the Early Years: Working Collaboratively for Children*. London: Paul Chapman Publishing.

Sobell, D. (1990) 'A place in the world: Adults' memories of childhood's special places.' *Children's Environments Quarterly*, 7(4).

Sobell, D. (1996). *Beyond Ecophobia: Reclaiming the Heart of Nature Education*. Great Barrington, MA: The Orion Society.

Sobell, D. (2002) *Children's Special Places: Exploring the Role of Forts, Dens and Bush Houses in Middle Childhood*. Detroit: Wayne State University Press.

Solly, K. (2002) Unpublished MA Thesis. University of North London with Pen Green.

Stephenson, A. (2003) 'Physical risk-taking: dangerous or endangered?' *Early Years* 23(1): 35–43.

Stonehouse, A. (Ed.) (1988) *Trusting Toddlers: Programming for 1–3 Year Olds in Child Care Centres*. Canberra: Australian Early Childhood Association.

Sylva, K., Melhuish, E., Sammons, P., Siraj-Blatchford, I. and Taggart, B. (2004) *The Effective Provision of Pre-School Education (EPPE) Technical Paper 1: The Final Report*. London: DfES/Institute of Education, University of London.

Tandy, C.A. (1999) 'Children's diminishing playspace: a study of intergenerational change in children's use of their neighbourhoods.' *Australian Geographical Studies*, 37(2): 154–64.

Teachers.org (2009) *The Learning Outside the Classroom Manifesto*. Available at: www.teachers.org.uk/files/OUTSIDE-CLASSROOM-manifesto.doc.

Theobalds, P. (1990) *The Teddy Bears Great Expedition*. London: Blackie.

Thomas, G. and Thompson, J. (2004) *A Child's Place: Why Environment Matters to Children*. London: Green Alliance/Demos. Available at: http://www.demos.co.uk/files/AChildsPlace.pdf.

Tickell, C. (2011) *The Early Years: Foundations for Life, Health and Learning*. Available at: www.education.gov.uk.

Titman, W. (1994) *Special Places, Special People: The Hidden Curriculum of School Grounds*. London: WWF UK/Learning Through Landscapes.

Tovey, H. (2007) *Playing Outdoors: Spaces and Places, Risk and Challenge*. Maidenhead: Open University Press.

Tulley, G. (2007) 'Geever Tulley on Five Dangerous Things for Kids.' Available at: www.ted.com/talks/geever-tulley-on-5-dangerous-things-for-kids.html.

UK National Statistics (2014) 'Leading causes of death by age group and sex.' Available at: http://www.statistics.gov.uk/hub/health-social-care/health-of-the-population/causes-of-death.

UNESCO (2014) 'United Nations decade of education for sustainable development (2005–2014).' Available at: unesdoc.unesco.org/images/0014/001416/141629e.pdf.

Valentine, G. (1997) 'Oh yes I can, oh no you can't: Children and parents understanding of kids competence to negotiate public space safely.' *Antipode*, 29(1): 65–89.

Vygotsky, L.S. (1962) *Thoughts and Language*. London: MIT Press and Wiley and Sons.

Vygotsky, L.S. (1978) *Mind in Society*. Cambridge, MA: Harvard University Press.

Walkerdine, V. (1996) 'Girls and boys in the classroom' in A. Pollard (Ed.), *Readings for Reflective Teaching in Primary Schools*. London: Cassell, pp. 298–300.

Watts, A. (2011) *Every Nursery Needs a Garden*. Abingdon: Routledge.

Ward Thompson, C., Aspinall, P. and Montarzino, A. (2008) 'The childhood factor: adult visits green places and the significance of childhood experience.' *Environment and Behaviour*, 40(1): 111–43.

Warden, C. (1999) *Outdoor Play*. Perthshire: Mindstretchers.

Warden, C. (2010) *Nature Kindergartens*. Perthshire: Mindstretchers.

Weber, L. (1971) *The English Infant School and Informal Education*. Upper Saddle River, NJ: Prentice Hall Inc.

Wells, N.M. and Evans, G.W. (2003) 'Nearly nature: a buffer of life stress among rural children.' *Environment and Behaviour*, 35(3): 311–30.

Welsh Assembly Government (2008) *Framework For Children's Learning For 3 to 7 Year-Olds in Wales*. Available at: www.wales.gov.uk.

White, J. (2008) *Playing and Learning Outdoors*. Abingdon: Routledge.

White, J. (2014) 'Vision and values.' Available at: www.janwhitenaturalplay.wordpress.com/visionand-values.

Wilkinson, R. (1980) *Questions and Answers on Rudolf Steiner Education*. East Grinstead: Henry Goulden.

Wilson, R.A. (1997) 'The wonders of nature: honoring children's way of knowing.' *Early Childhood News*, 6(9).

Wilson, R. (2007) *Nature and Young Children: Encouraging Creative Play and Learning in Natural Environments*. Abingdon: Routledge.

Wilson Smith, A. (2008) *Nature's Playthings*. Ludlow: Merlin Unwin Books.

Bibliography

Wood, D. (1988) *How Children Think and Learn: The Social Contexts of Cognitive Development* (2nd edition). Oxford: Blackwell.

Yerkes, J. (1982) cited in Bullard, J. (2010) *Outdoor Environments for Children*. Boston, MA: Pearson Allyn & Bacon/ Prentice Hall.

Sources of information and ideas

www.playengland.org.uk: Managing Risk in Play Provision

www.londonsdc.org/documents/SowingtheSeeds: Greater London Authority 2001

www.youngfoundation.org

www.ipaworls.org: International Play Association

cpis@ncb.org.uk: Children's Play Information Service

www.playengland.org.uk

www.lotc.org.uk

www.ltl.org.uk

www.rospa.co.uk/playsafet

www.earlyeducation.org.uk

www.ncrne.org.uk

www.nass.org.uk

http://schoolsensorygardens.co.uk

www.woodworks.wordpress.com

www.playpods.co.uk

www.rhs.org.uk

www.freeplaynetwork.org.uk

Resources and equipment

www.cosyfund.co.uk

www.communityplaythings.co.uk

www.tts.co.uk

www.earlyearsdirect.co.uk

www.mindstretchers.co.uk

www.sensetoys.com

www.soundchildren.com

www.childsplay.com

www.sirenfilmsco.uk

www.kozikidz.co.uk

www.sunproof.co.uk

Index

Index

Index

Index